Creating with Lace

Add the Personal Touch

Creating with Lace

Add the Personal Touch

MARY JO HINEY

Sterling Publishing Co., Inc. New York
A Sterling/Chapelle Book

Library of Congress Cataloging-in-Publication Data

Hiney, Mary Jo.
    Creating with lace : add the personal touch / Mary Jo Hiney.
        p.   cm.
    "A Sterling/Chapelle Book."
    Includes index.
    ISBN 0-8069-6299-2
    1. Lace   craft.   I.   Title.
TT810.H56   1999
746.2'2--dc21   99-35628
                                                                         CIP

10   9   8   7   6   5   4   3   2   1

Published by Sterling Publishing Company, Inc.
387 Park Avenue South, New York, N.Y. 10016
© 1999 by Chapelle Limited
Distributed in Canada by Sterling Publishing
c/o Canadian Manda Group, One Atlantic Avenue, Suite 105
Toronto, Ontario, Canada M6K 3E7
Distributed in Great Britain and Europe by Cassell PLC
Wellington House, 125 Strand, London WC2R 0BB, England
Distributed in Australia by Capricorn Link (Australia) Pty Ltd.
P.O. Box 6651, Baulkham Hills, Business Centre, NSW 2153, Australia
Printed in Hong Kong
All rights reserved

Sterling ISBN 0-8069-6299-2

For Chapelle Limited
Owner: Jo Packham
Editor: Ann Bear

Staff: Marie Barber, Areta Bingham,
Kass Burchett, Rebecca Christensen,
Brenda Doncouse, Dana Durney,
Marilyn Goff, Holly Hollingsworth,
Susan Jorgensen, Barbara Milburn,
Linda Orton, Karmen Quinney,
Leslie Ridenour, Cindy Stoeckl,
Gina Swapp

Photography: Kevin Dilley,
Photographer for Hazen Photography
Photo styling: Mary Jo Hiney

If you have any questions or
comments, please contact:
Chapelle, Ltd.
P.O. Box 9252
Ogden, UT 84409

(801) 621-2777
Fax (801) 621-2788
chapelle1@aol.com

To the ancient purpose of beauty that has been, is, and will be fostered through the gift of creativity.

It's hard for me to believe *Creating with Lace* is my ninth publication for Sterling/Chapelle. In 1991, I received a life-changing phone call from Jo Packham, who wondered if I would like to do some work for her. Jo has generously guided my career since then, and I would like to thank her for her belief in my capabilities. To my good friends and across-the-miles coworkers at Chapelle Ltd., I send my gratitude for many years of integrity-filled work done on my behalf, especially my editor Ann Bear for this current project. I am grateful to Sterling Publishing for their willingness to offer me the opportunity to express my creativity.

Among several industry-related companies, whose product contributions made this book feasible, I wish to thank Saro Trading Company for providing the beautiful linens, doilies, and laces that helped me create the book's flavor, and the Prym-Dritz Corporation for generously supplying me with plentiful amounts of Dylon Cold Water Fabric Dye, which allowed me to create a fresh appeal for classic goods.

I treasure the opportunity to write these books. I hope you will be inspired when you see the new textures and wonderful colors that can be expressed through a time-honored product.

Contents

A Place of Her Own

28

A Place for Holding Court

14

A Place for Renewal

58

A Place for
Good Company

76

A Place of Solitude

94

A Place to
Celebrate the Season

108

General Instructions

Introduction

As we have come to take for granted the benefits of the industrial revolution, and now the technical revolution, lace has become as every-day as a brown paper bag. But the legacy of lace goes far beyond that which is now available at the discount chain store.

The origin of lace is both royal and spiritual, its humble ancestry dating back to the 1400s. For many centuries, lace was made entirely by hand, produced by maidens whose efforts would yield an inch in an hour's time. During some of its history, lace was more precious than gold, and allowed to be worn only by the aristocracy.

Eventually, noisy, lumbering machines were devised to manufacture lace. For many laces, these same antiques are still employed to mass-produce today's openwork of ornamental design.

Treasured vintage laces are not inexpensive and each year, as supplies dwindle, they become more difficult to find. Which is one reason the heritage of fine lace or the legacy of machine-made lace can be used to take you to a time and create a place that is gracious, historical, personal, and memorable.

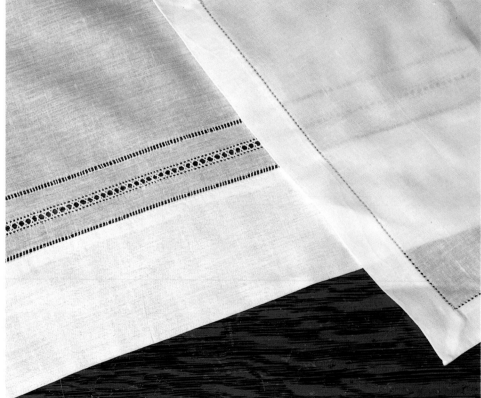

Almost all laces used in *Creating with Lace* are new and available at local retailers. As most pieces are made by hand, it is necessary that we acknowledge with gratitude the hands that have labored to provide for us these affordable items.

Creating with Lace invites you to look beyond lace as frothy and feminine and to see its amazing texture and its sometimes complicated, sometimes simplistic designs with a colorful new attitude. A new attitude that uses the most delicate of materials dyed in unexpected colors to create something extraordinary for someplace special, something cherished for someplace private, something new for someplace hidden.

Lace, whose history was to be made graciously by hand, can be that one hand-made, hand-dyed addition to your private sanctuary that transforms it into a place of self-expression and returns it to what belongs to only you.

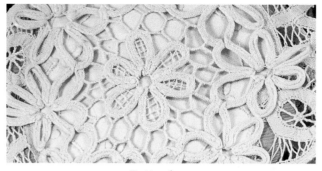

Battenburg

Cluny

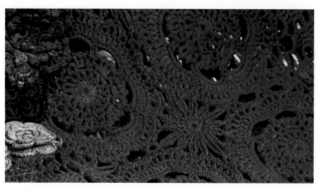

Crochet

Drawn Threadwork

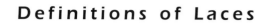

Definitions of Laces

Battenburg: A generalized definition used to describe any of the laces made from tape. It is done by basting machine-made braid or cord to a cloth or paper pattern and filling the spaces with a variety of lace stitches.

Cluny: A heavy bobbin lace with an open design, usually made of cotton threads, and named after its French town of origin, Cluny. Bobbin lace, now machine-produced, originally involved weaving many threads, wound on bobbins, into delicate and intricate designs.

Crochet: A delicate version of knitting, which uses a small hook to create lace-like designs through chain-stitch variations. English emigrants carried the craft to the New World, where it became a popular parlor art and represented a well-bred young woman's attributes. Irish Rose and Pineapple designs are two of many crocheted lace variations.

Drawn Threadwork: A technique in which some of the weft and warp threads are drawn from an evenweave fabric, then grouped together in a pattern. Hemstitching is the most common type of openwork in which threads are grouped with a drawn border and finished hem.

Filet Crochet: A chain-stitched square mesh pattern, where ornamental designs are created by filling specific spaces to form a motif. Filet crochet is a simplified version of the more difficult net lace known as filet.

Filet Crochet

Reticella: A type of needle lace, where a single thread and a single needle are used to produce designs of infinite complexity, then embroidered upon with exquisite variations of the buttonhole stitch.

Reticella

Tatting: A widespread, nineteenth-century pastime in which a fine lace was (and still is) made by looping and knotting thread that is wound on a hand shuttle. It is derived from macrame and most often worked with a fine cotton thread.

Tatting

Tuscany: An example of Victorian-American darned net—a derivative of macrame. Macrame is thought to have been developed by Middle Eastern carpet weavers. The craft was transported to the Tuscany region of fifteenth-century Italy, where it was called *punto a groppo,* or knotted points.

Tuscany

General Dyeing Instructions

From start to finish, the process of hand-dyeing is fun. Each step on the way leads to discovery.

As you will be working with a variety of natural fibers and several different types of linen or lace, the differences will cause some items to absorb dye more thoroughly than others. This, coupled with variable conditions when hand-dyeing in your home, will delight you with the spontaneity and custom-look of hand-dyed goods. Some color flexibility is helpful, as individual dyeing conditions will vary. Remember to prewash items prior to dyeing, so any finish on the item is removed.

Cold water, fiber-reactive dye was used for all hand-dyeing in *Creating with Lace* and comes in .2 oz. packages. Fiber-reactive dye is a type of dye composed of chemical qualities similar to those in natural fibers. When salt and fixative are added to the dye, a chemical reaction occurs and marries the dye to the fiber,

making colors permanent and colorfast. It is available at most craft or fabric stores.

Fiber-reactive dye is different from acid-dispersed dye, commonly found at grocery or drug stores. An acid-dispersed dye pushes itself onto the fiber surface, rather than integrating with the fiber.

Refer to Color Chart on page 13 for the specific dye colors used. In addition, these basic colors are mixed in "dye recipes" at the beginning of each chapter, to create new shades. As dye colors and names vary from brand to brand, you may want to make a color copy of the color chart to use as a reference when purchasing dyes. When less than a full package of dye is necessary, mix the whole package with water and divide the liquid portion required. Store remaining dye (without fixative added).

Not all fabrics are suitable for fiber-reactive dyes, as this dye reacts best chemically with natural fibers. Some suitable fabrics include cotton, linen, rayon, and silk. Nylon, acrylic, polyester, and other synthetic materials should be avoided.

Color Chart

- Primrose -
- Sahara Sun -
- Nasturtium -

- Mandarin -
- Mexican Red -
- Tahiti Rose -

- Radiant Pink -
- Purple Vine -
- Ultraviolet -

- Lilac -
- Riviera Blue -
- Sea Green -

- Leaf Green -
- Tartan Green -
- Café au Lait -

- Koala Brown -
- Bronze Rose -
- Black -

If the desired shade is critical, take time to test-dye a 12" square of untreated fabric. When wet, most fabric shades are two times darker than when dry. To check permanent color after dyeing, wash the test fabric in hot, soapy water and dry.

If color is not absolutely critical, use small swatches of white or beige cotton broadcloth to test dye bath colors before the dyeing process. Many of the new shades developed for this book are pastels, lights, or ice versions of the packaged dye. To achieve these pale shades, dilute the dye bath by using less dye and more water than is necessary to simply cover the items. Add water to dye bath in increments of 32 oz. A broadcloth test swatch can be used to determine if more water is necessary. Continue to add water until rinsed swatch is two times darker than the desired shade.

Because individual conditions may vary when hand-dyeing, be watchful and flexible with expected dye time. It is recommended that items remain in the dye bath for at least 30 minutes so the chemical reaction can occur.

Plan ahead if making several of the projects in a chapter. Dye as much as possible at one time. For your convenience, listed with each dye recipe are the projects for which it is used.

It is wise to be organized. Make a chart that lists

the items being dyed and the desired color. Separate items into color piles and label with the dye bath shade. Spend a day dyeing the items. For some shades, the complete dyeing process will take about two hours, including rinsing. Paler shades can take as little as 40 minutes.

For permanent colors, salt and dye fixative must be used. Once the salt and dye fixative are added to the dye bath, dyeing must take place immediately. Discard dye bath with fixative after use. It cannot be reused.

▪ General Dyeing Supplies ▪

Here is a basic list of supplies. As brands and individual circumstances may vary, the following list may need to be modified. Containers, measuring spoons, and other household items used for dyeing should be retired from food usage.

Bottle opener (some of the dyes come packaged in a small tin, others do not)

Containers (several 32 oz. size with measurement amounts labeled on side)

Dye fixative (included with fiber-reactive dye)

Fiber-reactive dye

Measuring spoons

Rubber gloves

Salt

Scissors: craft

Spoons (large and small for stirring)

Spray bottle (with water)

Tub (large or small tub depending on item sizes)

▪ Step by Step Dyeing Instructions ▪

The following measurements and instructions may vary depending on dye manufacturer.

1 Before prewashing any linen or lace prior to dyeing, weigh items dry and make a note of it. Each .2 oz. package of dye will color up to 8 oz. of dry fabric weight. Refer to Dyeing Small Quantities on page 17 if the total weight is less than 8 oz. Wash

and rinse all selected items (preshrink). Small quantities may be washed in a small tub. Do not use fabric softener. Leave damp and set aside. **2** Fill large container with enough cold water to cover selected items. **3** Wearing rubber gloves, open dye package. Place dye in measuring cup and add 2 cups of warm water. Stir until dissolved. Add dissolved dye to container of water, stir well. Use the full amount of dissolved dye whenever possible. Repeat for each shade of dye required. Clean up after each shade, as the particles of dye may have found their way into unfortunate places. **4** Place 4 Tbs. salt and one package dye fixative in measuring cup for each .2 oz. dye package to be used. Add 2 cups hot tap water. Stir until dissolved. Add dissolved fixative to dye in container and stir well. Repeat for each shade of dye required. Use fabric swatch to test dye bath shade. Add water as necessary for pastels, lights, and ice shades. **5** Place damp item(s) in dye bath. Stir or agitate item continuously for 10 minutes, then

stir occasionally for 50 minutes, unless otherwise noted in dye bath recipes. Keep fabric submerged. **6** Rinse until water becomes clear. Wash in very hot water with detergent; rinse again. Use a washing machine for this step, if possible. Very small pieces can be placed into a small fabric or mesh bag and then washed. **7** Lay items flat to dry. Use terry cloth towels as a surface on which to lay items, helping to absorb moisture. Press while still slightly damp. Mist with water if necessary to remove wrinkles.

▪ Dyeing Small Quantities ▪

Choose the option of mixing a small dye bath if the items being dyed are less than 8 oz. of dry weight. Because the dye, when dry, is a combination of many different shades, the full package of dye must be prepared, or an unexpected shade of dye may dominate. Mix dye in 32 oz. container (container should have measurement amounts labeled on the side). Once a smaller dye bath has been prepared (without fixative), seal and label excess dye. For smaller dye baths, use measuring spoons to determine the amount of fixative to be mixed. The dye bath with fixative must be used within one hour of mixing. Store unmixed package of fixative near mixed dye for later use.

Some dyes for smaller quantities are available in small plastic squeeze bottles and have a paint consistency. The dyes may be mixed directly on the item, and as little as one small doily can be dyed. The item will need to be heat-set.

1 Wet the item to be dyed, then blot out moisture. **2** Shake dye bottle and squeeze a small amount of dye onto the item. Use a paintbrush to work dye into fibers. **3** Heat-set, then rinse and press.

A third alternative for dyeing small quantities is to use a high-quality acrylic paint mixed with fabric medium and water. Refer to Fabric Paints on page 19 for more information.

1 Thin the paint to a sprayable consistency. **2** Pour diluted paint into a small spray bottle, then mist to color item. A paintbrush can also be used to brush diluted paint onto item. **3** Heat set item.

Many retailers sell silk dyes in small bottles. Silk dyes are formulated for protein-based fibers, such as silk and wool. Although linen is also a protein-based fiber, most of the linens and laces used in *Creating with Lace* are either cotton or combinations of linen and cotton; and as such, it would be safer to use the fiber-reactive dyes.

Decoupage with Fabrics & Laces

Several projects in *Creating with Lace* use decoupage medium and tacky glue to adhere lace or fabric to papier maché or wood for a beautiful effect. When decoupaging, always have wet and dry rags on hand for keeping hands clean. Work on a protected work surface. A paper bag torn open at the seams makes an excellent drop cloth and provides for simple and quick clean-up.

▪ General Decoupage Supplies ▪

Decoupage medium	Paper bag drop cloth
Paint roller: 3"-wide, disposable	Paper towels
Paint tray: small	Sponge
Paintbrush: 1"-wide, flat	Tacky glue: thin bodied

▪ General Decoupage Instructions ▪

1 Pour a small amount of tacky glue into paint tray. Roll thin, even coat onto paint roller. Apply to wrong side of lace, being careful to keep glue from right side of lace. Position lace on papier maché or wood object. Smooth lace into place. **2** Using paintbrush, apply thin coat of decoupage medium over top of lace and papier maché or wood object. Use paper towels to blot decoupage medium so that it penetrates lace fibers and does not remain only on lace surface or puddle at lace edges. Let dry. Apply second coat of decoupage medium.

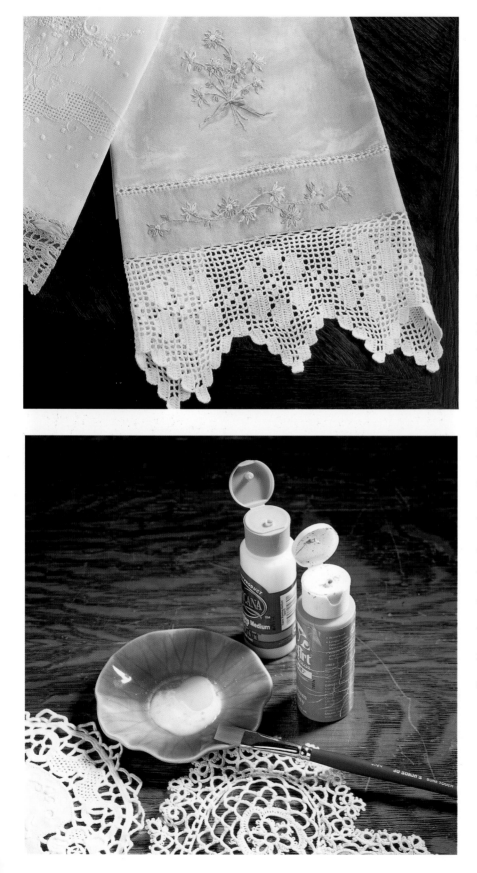

Fabric Paints

Many quality fabric paints are available at fabric and craft stores. Depending on the manufacturer, the quality and consistency may vary in color and finish. Some fabric paints may leave lace or linens stiff, while others may not. Thinning paint with fabric medium and water will help eliminate some stiffness created by some paints. Metallic and pearlescent paints formulated for fabric can be used to enhance a theme, such as Christmas.

When finished painting, let item dry, then heat-set with an iron. The item may be washed in warm, soapy water and pressed while slightly damp for a permanent and completely washable finish.

Fabric Stamping

Stamping on fabric is a popular way to add color and distinctiveness to any project. The stamp creates an outline and fabric ink or permanent pens complete the look. Choose rubber stamps that are not extremely detailed as the detail will not translate to fabric.

Most fabric inks and pens must be heat-set to be permanent. Fabric pens are available with different sized brush tips for fine detailing and filling in color. They also come in a wide variety of colors including fluorescent, metallic, and pastels. A round fabric scrubber brush or a stencil brush is useful for coloring areas of the stamped image without concealing the design's details.

Use a piece of cardboard, such as the back of a pad of paper, as a work surface cushion when stamping. Avoid corrugated cardboard.

Keeping stamps clean is very important. Place stamps on several layers of damp paper towels on a plastic plate, and have another plate handy with several dry paper towels.

▪ General Fabric Stamping Supplies ▪

Fabric ink

Fabric ink stamp pad

Fabric markers: fine tipped; medium tipped

Round fabric scrubber brush: 2/0 or Stencil brush: ¼"

Rubber stamp

Rubber stamp cleaner

▪ General Fabric Stamping Instructions ▪

1 To ink stamp, place stamp on work surface, rubber die side up. Firmly press fabric ink pad onto rubber die so that entire surface is covered, but not oozing with ink. **2** Test the inked image on a scrap of fabric to determine the amount of hand pressure the stamp will need and how long hand pressure should be applied (time will vary from three to twenty seconds). **3** Plan spacing of stamped images before stamping. **4** To color in areas of the stamped design, use fabric ink pad as "paint." Dab scrubber brush on ink pad. Remove excess ink on a dry paper towel. Using a swirling motion, lightly ink small sections of the design. **5** To emphasize the detail of a stamped outline, use a fine point fabric marker to retrace image. **6** When finished using stamp, blot stamp on damp paper towels on plate. Rub stamp cleaner over stamp and blot again. Repeat until stamp is clean and blot stamp on dry paper towels.

Battings

Batting is traditionally used as the middle layer of a quilt or sometimes in clothing, doll making, and certain other crafts. There are numerous types of batting available. Bonded cotton batting gives a flat, natural appearance and will require a great deal of quilting to secure layers, with quilting lines less than 1" apart. When laundered, heirloom cotton batting will shrink, producing a vintage appearance on a quilt. Felt or needle punch batting may be substituted and renders the same appearance as bonded cotton although heavier in weight. Polyester batting gives a puffy appearance.

Tip: Remove batting from the package a day before using. Open it out to full size. This will help the batting lay flat.

Pillow Forms

Several projects in *Creating with Lace* require pillow forms. Creating custom pillow forms is easy and quick.

1 Cut a piece of fabric that is double the width of the pillow, plus 1½", and the height of the pillow plus 1½". **2** Fold length of fabric in half, matching width edges. Beginning at fold, sew outside edges, taking a ½" seam allowance and leaving the remaining width edge open. **3** Turn right side out. Stuff firmly. Sew or hand-stitch open edge closed, turning raw edges under ½".

Overlapping Laces

When sewing laces or linens together for a collage, overlap one finished edge ¼" onto other linen or lace. Use a narrow zigzag stitch to sew laces together. If possible, sew a second time ⅛" to ¼" away from first row of stitching. Trim away underlapping linen or lace close to second row of stitching, eliminating the muddled appearance that may be caused by overlapped laces.

For garment assembly, use a narrow zigzag stitch to machine-sew doilies or laces together. The zigzag stitch creates "give" and also camouflages the stitches.

Window Coverings

Windows come in endless shapes and sizes. Additionally, individual tastes vary in the fullness of the gathers desired for window coverings. Some prefer flat texture or lace treatments. Others prefer window coverings that are quite full. Individually modify the curtains and valances in *Creating with Lace* to suit your taste.

Make additional adjustments if a larger or smaller rod pocket is required. A larger tablecloth or longer table runner may be a more pleasing choice for your window. Consider using lace trim as a bridge between linen towels or table runners in order to increase the overall size of linen or lace items. Whatever options you decide upon, choosing lacy linens for window coverings will prove a simple task and a graceful addition to your home.

Embellishments

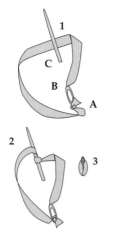

▪ Bullion Lazy Daisy ▪

1 Bring needle up at A. Keep ribbon flat, untwisted, and full. Go down through fabric at B and up at C, but do not pull through. **2** Snugly wrap ribbon around needle tip one to three times. Holding finger over wrapped ribbon, pull needle through ribbon and go down through fabric close to C. **3** Completed Bullion Lazy Daisy.

▪ Buttonhole Stitch ▪

1 Bring needle up at A, go down at B and up at C, looping thread under needle. Continue for desired length of stitching, keeping needle vertical. **2** Completed Buttonhole Stitch.

▪ Colonial Knot ▪

1 Bring needle up at A. Drape ribbon in a backward "C". Place needle through "C". **2** Wrap ribbon over needle and under tip of the needle forming a figure-8. Hold ribbon firmly on needle. Go down through fabric close to A. Hold ribbon securely until knot is formed on top of fabric. **3** Completed Colonial Knot.

▪ Cross-stitch ▪

1 Stitches are done in a row or, if necessary, one at a time in an area. Bring needle up at A and go down at B. Come up at C and go down at D, etc. **2** Completed top stitches create "X". All top stitches should lie in the same direction. Come up at E and go down at F, etc.

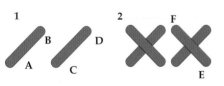

■ Doily Rosette ■

1 Fold doily in half, then in thirds. **2** Fold bottom corner over. Glue bottom folded corner to hold it in place. Place thin bead of glue at center of second doily. Hand-stitch first doily into center of second doily. Fold second doily up around first doily to slightly ruffle. **3** Completed Doily Rosette.

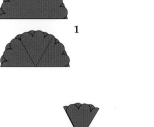
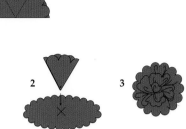

■ Folded Leaf ■

1 Fold each end of ribbon length forward diagonally. **2** Gather-stitch across bottom edge of folds. **3** Tightly pull gather thread and knot for a completed Folded Leaf.

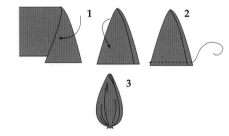

■ Gathered Petal ■

1 Cut ribbon into required lengths. Gather-stitch bottom and side edges. Tightly pull thread and knot. **2** Completed Gathered Petal.

■ Gathered Ribbon Ruffle ■

1 Fold length of ribbon in half, matching width ends. Gather-stitch along one selvage edge. Tightly gather and secure thread. **2** Completed Gathered ribbon ruffle.

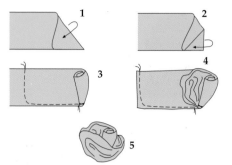

▪ Gathered Rosebud ▪

1 Fold end of ribbon diagonally. **2** Fold diagonal end in half. **3** Roll folded end and secure at bottom of roll. Gather-stitch opposite end. **4** Tightly gather to form petal and secure thread. Wrap gathered petal around center roll to form bud. **5** Completed Gathered Rosebud.

▪ Lazy Daisy ▪

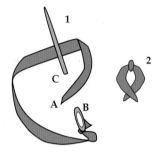

1 Bring needle up at A. Keep ribbon flat, untwisted, and full. Go down through fabric at B and up at C, keeping ribbon under needle to form a loop. Pull ribbon through, leaving loop loose and full. To hold loop in place, go down on other side of ribbon near C, forming a straight stitch over loop. **2** Completed Lazy Daisy.

▪ Outline Stitch ▪

1 Working from left to right, make slightly slanting stitches along the outline. Bring needle up at A, go down at B, keeping thread or ribbon to the right and above the needle. Come up at C (halfway between A and B). Make all stitches the same length. Go down at D (half the length of the stitch beyond B), and continue for desired length of stitching.

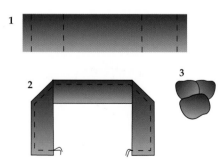

▪ Pansy ▪

1 Mark ribbon length into three intervals, as shown. **2** Fold ends down. Gather-stitch as shown. Pull thread to ruffle ribbon, forming petals. Join last petal to first, hiding raw edge. **3** Completed Pansy.

▪ Ribbon Stitch ▪

1 Bring needle up at A. Lay ribbon flat on fabric. At end of stitch, pierce ribbon with needle. Slowly pull length of ribbon through to back, allowing ends of ribbon to curl. If ribbon is pulled too tight, the effect may be lost. Vary petals and leaves by adjusting length, tension of ribbon before piercing, position of piercing, and how loosely or tightly ribbon is pulled down through itself. **2** Completed Ribbon Stitch.

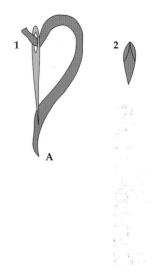

▪ Rosette ▪

1 Fold length of ribbon down at right angle, creating a post to hold onto. **2** Fold folded end in half. Sew in place. **3** Roll and fold ribbon, holding post. Sew to secure. **4** When ribbon is rolled and folded half its length, hand-stitch a gathering stitch along the bottom edge of remaining length of ribbon. Tightly pull gathering stitch and wrap gathered section around folded rosette. Sew in place to secure. **5** Completed Rosette.

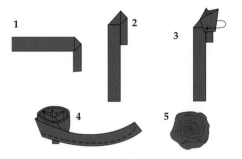

▪ Ruched Ribbon Stitch ▪

1 Bring ribbon up at A. Fray loose end of ribbon and pull one center fiber to gather ribbon. Move gathers down ribbon to entry point. **2** Adjust gathers to stitch length. Pierce center of ribbon at B and pull through. **3** Completed Ruched Ribbon Stitch.

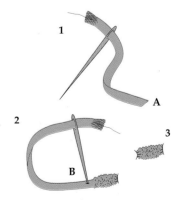

A Place of Her Own

When creating a place for someone else—someone young, someone that you love—let it be an honest statement about who she is, yet whimsical enough to fulfill her dream of an enchanting "secret garden" all her own. Echo her view that everyday life is a fanciful journey. Fill her place with lace flowers of a most delicate coloring and such unexpected things as a birdhouse lamp. Her place should possess an attitude about decorating that literally celebrates the constant joys and inspirations of youth and springtime.

However, the place that you create for her must also offer comfort and utility, as well as a true sense of color and style. It should be a quiet setting that can replenish her soul, a creative environment of undefined good taste, yet a "day-to-day" place for making her feel she is truly a part of what she calls home.

Dye Recipes

▪ Sea Green ▪

Leave in dye bath 30 minutes.

.2 oz. Sea Green

Used with Lacy Socks on page 37.

▪ Lilac ▪

Leave in dye bath 30 minutes.

.2 oz. Lilac

Used with Patch Quilt on page 39; Small Purse on page 33; Toddler Bonnet on page 42; Window Shade & Valance on page 31.

▪ Orchid ▪

Diluted dye bath. Leave in dye bath 30 minutes.

.1 oz. Lilac (8 oz. mixed)

.1 oz. Purple Vine (8 oz. mixed)

Used with Bright Pillows on page 38; Lacy Socks on page 37; Patch Quilt on page 39; Small Purse on page 33; Toddler Bonnet on page 42.

▪ Leaf Green ▪

Diluted dye bath. Leave in dye bath 30 minutes.

.1 oz. Leaf Green (8 oz. mixed)

Used with Bright Pillows on page 38; Lacy Socks on page 37; Patch Quilt on page 39; Small Purse on page 33; Toddler Bonnet on page 42.

▪ Mandarin ▪

Diluted dye bath. Leave in dye bath 30 minutes.

.1 oz. Mandarin (8 oz. mixed)

Used with Doll Bed on page 40; Lacy Socks on page 37; Night Light on page 34; Patch Quilt on page 39; Small Purse on page 33; Toddler Bonnet on page 42.

▪ Sahara Sun ▪

Diluted dye bath. For paler shade, use very diluted dye bath. Leave in dye bath 30 minutes.

.05 oz. Sahara Sun (4 oz. mixed)

Use with Doll Bed on page 40; Lacy Socks on page 37; Patch Quilt on page 39; Table Drape on page 36; Toddler Bonnet on page 42; Window Shade & Valance on page 31.

Window Shade & Valance

Supplies
(for a small window)

Fiber-reactive dyes: (.05 oz.) Sahara Sun; (.2 oz) Lilac

Lace trim: (1½ yd.) 6"-wide, filet crochet

Linen towels: (2) 28" x 44", White with Cluny lace trim

Roller shade kit

1 Refer to General Dyeing Instructions on page 12 and Dye Recipes on page 30. Prepare dye baths. Dye towels Lilac and trim Sahara Sun. Press all items while slightly damp. **2** Refer to Window Coverings on page 23. Fuse roller shade backing material to towel. Trim backing material flush to shaped edge of towel. Pin and sew trim to bottom of towel, using a narrow zigzag stitch, centering trim motif with towel center. Hem side edges of towel. Assemble roller shade kit, following manufacturer's instructions. **3** Trim second towel to dimensions desired for a flat valance. Fuse backing fabric to valance towel. Pin and sew trim to bottom of towel with a narrow zigzag stitch. Hem side edges of towel. **4** Fold and sew raw edge of valance under, forming a rod pocket.

Rosebud Boutonniere

Supplies (for one)

Florist tape: (12") ½"-wide, Green

Florist wire: (4") 40-gauge, Green

Lace doilies: 2" square; 2" heart, Battenburg

Leaf: 1½"–2"-wide, Green, silk

Ribbon: (6") 1½"-wide, bright color

1 Bend a small loop at one end of florist wire. Refer to Gathered Rosebud on page 26. Make first fold of rosebud from ribbon. Place loop near center bottom edge of rosebud fold. Finish rosebud, sewing florist wire to ribbon through loop. Finish rosebud. **2** Wrap stitched edge of rosebud and top 1" of florist wire with florist tape. **3** Cut center from doilies, creating ¾"-wide center openings. Gather-stitch around centers. Slip wired rosebud through center of square doily. Pull gather thread as tight as possible so doily gathers around rosebud. Wrap thread several times around rosebud and knot. Shape doily "petals."

Repeat with heart doily, offsetting petals. **4** Wrap florist wire with florist tape, beginning just below heart doily. Position leaf under heart doily. Continue wrapping florist wire with florist tape. Tie small bow with ribbon and adhere to bottom edge of heart doily near leaf. To coil stem, wrap taped florist wire around crochet hook or other narrow round item.

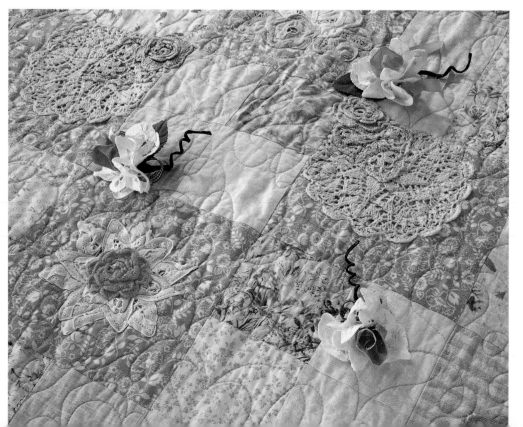

Supplies

Batting: 12" x 8", lightweight

Button; 1" multicolored, novelty

Cording; (1⅛ yd.) ¼"-wide,
    Light Purple

Cotton fabric: 13" x 8",
    Orange/multicolored, plaid
    seersucker; 13" x 11",
    multicolored, print

Crocheted flowers: (9) 3",
    White; (4) 2" White

Fiber-reactive dyes: (.1 oz.)
    Mandarin; (.2 oz. each) Leaf
    Green; Purple Vine;
    (.3 oz.) Lilac

Small Purse

1 Refer to General Dyeing Instructions on page 12 and Dye Recipes on page 30. Prepare dye baths. Dye three 3" flowers Mandarin, three 3" flowers Leaf Green, three 3" flowers Lilac, and 2" flowers Orchid. Press all items while slightly damp. **2** Cut 13" x 3" strip from print fabric. **3** Fold plaid fabric in half lengthwise with right sides together. Sew raw width edges together, taking ½" seam allowance, forming a tube. Press seam open. Repeat with 13" x 8" print fabric for lining. Turn lining right side out. Position seams at center of tube. Slip purse over lining, right sides together, matching center seams, and raw edges. Fold batting around tubes, aligning batting with bottom purse edge. Batting will extend ½" above top purse edge. Hand-stitch batting edges together. **4** Sew purse bottom through all six layers, taking ½" seam allowance. Trim seam to ¼". Turn purse right side out, press. Mark purse sides at top inside edges. Pin and baste cording ends to purse at marks. **5** Fold 3" x 13" print fabric piece in half widthwise. Sew raw width edges together, taking a ½" seam allowance. Press seam open. Bind top edge of purse with print fabric strip, working from plaid side and taking a ½" seam allowance around purse opening. Press strip towards batting. Fold strip over to inside. Turn raw edge of strip under ¼" and sew in place. **6** Pin flowers onto purse front, overlapping the flowers in color rows. Hand-stitch to purse front. Hand-stitch button to purse front.

Night Light

Supplies

Braid: (½ yd.) ¼"-wide
  Pink/Blue check

Elastic: (3½") ⅜"-wide

Fabric paint: Lime; Orchid

Fabrics: (six styles, ¼ yd. each)
  cotton print; (⅓ yd. for
  lampshade) cotton print

Fiber-reactive dye: (.2 oz)
  Mandarin

Lace table runner: 16" x 36",
  White

Lace trims: (two styles, ½ yd.
  each) ¼"-wide, White, tatted

Lamp

Lampshade: 5"-diameter, Ivory

Ribbon: (1½ yd.) ⅜"-wide
  Orange/Red plaid

1 Cut table runner in half to measure 8" x 36". Preshrink half of table runner. **2** Refer to General Dyeing Instructions on page 12 and Dye Recipes on page 30. Prepare dye bath and dye preshrunk half of table runner Mandarin. Press while slightly damp. **3** Refer to Decoupage with Fabric & Laces on page 18. Trace lampshade on wrong side of one print fabric, adding ½" all around to traced shape. Decoupage fabric to lampshade, adhering edges to inside of shade. **4** Fold and press cut edge of Mandarin table runner under 1½" to wrong side. Sew ½" from fold. Sew again ⅝" from previous stitching, turning raw edge under while sewing. On right side, topstitch ribbon over casing on top of previous stitching. Insert elastic through casing. Fit cover to lampshade, tightening elastic as necessary, and so that table runner ends overlap at center back. Seam elastic. Tie bow from remaining ribbon and tack to lampshade cover at center front. **5** Cut fabrics to cover lamp base as desired. Fabric pieces should overlap by ¼" at every other section. For the remaining sections, cut fabric close to an exact fit, trimming to shape as necessary. Decoupage fabrics onto lamp base, overlapping and trimming fabric where necessary. Paint one lace trim Lime and second Orchid. Let dry. Decoupage braid and lace trims onto lamp base to accent shapes. **6** Apply thin coat of decoupage medium to lamp base. Rub decoupage medium along cut edges to eliminate fabric frays. Let dry; sand. Apply several coats of decoupage medium. Sand between coats when dry.

Table Drape

Supplies

Fiber-reactive dye: (.05 oz.)
   Sahara Sun

Lace table topper: 36" square,
   filet crochet

1 Refer to General Dyeing Instructions on page 12 and Dye Recipes on page 30. Prepare dye bath and dye table topper Sahara Sun. Press while slightly damp. **2** Cover table with table topper as desired.

Lacy Socks

1 Refer to General Dyeing Instructions on page 12 and Dye Recipes on page 30. Prepare dye baths. Dye one pair of socks Leaf Green, second pair of socks Sahara Sun, 1½" trim Mandarin, one style ½" trim Sea Green, and second style ½" trim Orchid. Let socks dry. Press laces while slightly damp. **2** Cut 1½" trim in half. Fold each cut piece in half with right sides together. Sew ends. Press seams open. Sew a trim to each cuff edge of Leaf Green socks, right sides together, with narrow zigzag stitch. Stretch cuff edge while sewing so that lace trim fits cuff edge. Fold lace down. Sew ½" trims to Sahara Sun socks, one slightly above the other.

Supplies (for two)

Cotton socks: (2 pair) White

Fiber-reactive dyes:
    (.05 oz.) Sahara Sun;
    (.1 oz.) Mandarin;
    (.2 oz. each) Leaf Green; Sea
    Green; Lilac; Purple Vine

Lace trim: (27" each) 1½"-wide
    White, Cluny; (two styles)
    ½"-wide, White, tatted

Bright Pillows

Supplies (for two)

Fiber-reactive dyes: (.2 oz. each) Leaf Green; Lilac; Purple Vine

Lace pillowcases: (2) 20" x 30", White, Cluny

Ribbons: (1 yd.) ¼"-wide, Peach/White checkered, French braid; (1 yd.) ¼"-wide, Pink with Cream butterflies, French braid; (½ yd.) ½"-wide, Pale Yellow/Orchid, grosgrain

1 Refer to General Dyeing Instructions on page 12 and Dye Recipes on page 30. Prepare dye baths. Dye one pillowcase Leaf Green and second pillowcase Orchid. Press while slightly damp. **2** Refer to Pillow Forms on page 22. Separate pillowcase front from back. Use pillowcase back to make pillow form for contrasting pillow. **3** Trim Orchid pillowcase front to 18" x 27½". Trim Leaf Green pillowcase front to 16" x 27½".

Using checkered braid on Leaf Green pillow and butterfly braid on Orchid pillow, sew one row of braid next to edge of pillow's lace trim, using a narrow zigzag stitch. Repeat with grosgrain ribbon, adjoining braid and grosgrain edges. Finish with a second row of braid. Press after each trim has been sewn in place. **4** Overlap straight edge of lace on each pillowcase front ½" onto cut edge of fabric, forming a tube with right side out. Sew at overlap, 2" in from both side edges, leaving a large opening. Turn pillow inside out and align side edges, making certain lace edge is 1½" from one folded edge. Sew side edges together, taking a ½" seam allowance. Turn pillow right side out through opening. Make pillow form. Insert form into pillow. Hand-stitch opening closed.

Supplies

Batting: queen-size, heirloom cotton

Cotton Fabric: (7 yds. total, various complementary prints) 44"-wide; (6 yds.) solid or soft print (for quilt back)

Fiber-reactive dyes:
(.05 oz.) Sahara Sun; (.2 oz. each) Leaf Green; Sea Green; Lilac; Mandarin; Purple Vine

Lace doilies: various

Lace motifs: various

Lace trim: (7 yds.) 4"-wide, White

Patch Quilt

1 Refer to General Dyeing Instructions on page 12 and Dye Recipes on page 30. Prepare Sea Green, Mandarin, Leaf Green, Lilac, Sahara Sun and Orchid dye baths. Dye doilies and lace as desired. Press all items while slightly damp. **2** Make patchwork quilt top as desired. Sew doilies and motifs to quilt as desired. Machine-quilt top, batting, and backing together. Machine-wash quilt in cold water, dry in dryer. Batting will shrink, creating an antique look. **3** Bind quilt edges, using 1¼"-wide fabric strips. Designate one end of the quilt as top. Sew lace trim over binding, working from top side, leaving lace off top edge. Lace trim is gathered around corners. Hem lace ends. Hand-stitch additional doilies to quilt top as desired.

39

Doll Bed

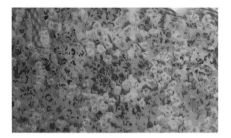

Supplies

Batting: (½ yd.) lightweight

Crocheted flowers: (4) 3",
White; (10) 1", White

Decoupage medium: Clear

Fabrics: (seven styles, ⅓ yd.
each) 44"-wide, bright
florals, cotton print; (one
small square) White, felt

Fiber-reactive dyes: (.05 oz.)
Sahara Sun; (.2 oz. each) Sea
Green; Mandarin; (premixed
for small quantities) Blue;
Orange; Periwinkle; Yellow

Flowers: (2) 4" x 5", White,
Belgian lace

Lace trim: (2¼ yds.) 3"-wide,
White, crocheted

Linen placemats: (2) 14" x 20",
White, embroidered

Motifs: various (in pairs)

Polyester stuffing: handful

Wooden doll bed: 15" x 10",
unfinished

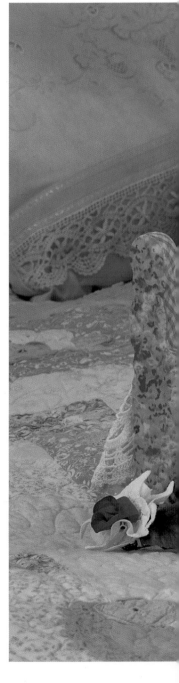

1 Refer to General Dyeing Instructions on page 12 and Dye Recipes on page 30. Prepare dye baths. Dye one placemat Sahara Sun, second placemat Mandarin, two 3" flowers Leaf Green, two 3" flowers Sea Green, one 4" x 5" flower Lilac and second Blue, and motifs in pairs as desired. Overdye scalloped edge of lace trim Yellow. Press all items while slightly damp. **2** Refer to Decoupage with Fabric & Laces on page 18 and Night Light on page 34. Decoupage fabrics to bed as desired, using same method as for Night Light. Apply thin coat of decoupage medium to entire bed. Rub decoupage medium along cut edges to eliminate fabric frays. Sand when dry. Apply several coats of decoupage medium. Sand between coats when dry. **3** For com-forter, pin and sew lace trim to scalloped edge of Sahara Sun placemat, trimming bulk at corners. Cut batting ⅛" smaller all around than placemat. Layer batting, Sahara Sun placemat, and Mandarin placemat. Pin and machine-quilt layers together with wrong sides together. Use extra batting for mattress and bed pillow. **4** For throw pillows, hand-stitch Leaf Green flowers together at edges, leaving a small opening. Fill with polyester stuffing, then sew opening closed. Repeat with Sea Green flowers and Periwinkle flowers. Cut felt pieces the same size as each motif. Sew felt to wrong side of motifs, leaving an opening. Fill with polyester stuffing, then sew opening closed. Cut two 3½" circles from fabric scrap. Sew edges with right sides together, leaving an opening. Turn right side out through opening. Fill with polyester stuffing, then sew opening closed. Tack or adhere 1" flowers to outer edge of round pillow.

Toddler Bonnet

Note: It may be necessary to increase or decrease the amount of flowers used for a proper fit. Be certain to measure child's head before purchasing items.

Supplies

Crocheted doilies: 12", White, round; 4" White, round

Crocheted flowers: (16) 3", White; (5) 2", White; (8) 2", Beige

Fabric stiffener: 4 oz.

Fiber-reactive dyes: (.05 oz.) Sahara Sun; (.1 oz. each) Leaf Green; Purple Vine; (.2 oz) Mandarin: (.3 oz.) Lilac

1 Refer to General Dyeing Instructions on page 12 and Dye Recipes on page 30. Prepare dye baths. Dye 12" doily Sahara Sun, 4" doily Mandarin, eight 3" flowers Leaf Green, remaining 3" flowers Lilac, and 2" White flowers Orchid. Press while slightly damp. **2** Sew 4" doily to center of 12" doily with narrow zigzag stitch. Sew one 2" Orchid flower to center of 4" doily. At outer edge of 12" doily, sew ½"–¾"-deep tucks at each scallop, adjusting amount to fit head size. **3** Sew or hand-stitch 3" Leaf Green flowers together, sewing two petals of each flower to each adjoining flower, forming a ring. Overlap and sew ring to outer edge of 12" doily. This forms bonnet crown. **4** For bonnet brim, sew or hand-stitch 3" Lilac flowers together, aligning and joining one petal each time. Before joining first flower to last, steam press the brim so it curves and causes outer edge to become wider than inner edge. Along inner edge, position and sew 2" Beige flowers, overlapping joined sections of Lilac flowers onto Beige flowers. Overlap and sew Lilac/Beige brim onto Leaf Green bottom edge of crown. **5** On Lilac outer edge, position and sew one Orchid flower in-between each of four joined Wisteria flowers, designating this Orchid-trimmed edge as bonnet front. Sew a ½"-deep tuck at brim center, bringing Lilac center flower up onto a Leaf Green flower. **6** Stiffen bonnet with fabric stiffener. Place bonnet crown over small inverted bowl, laying brim flat to dry. Bonnet will be starched but not stiff.

From the moment the announcement was made, the planning for the parties, showers, and wedding had begun. The place for all of these must be perfect. It must be an enchanting locale, a place outside where the smell of flowers in bloom and the songs of the birds can be enjoyed by everyone. This must be a place to hold court, a place where dreams come true, and promises are fulfilled.

The promise. The one between you and your daughter—the bride-to-be. The promise to always be there, whenever you should, to help create a place that celebrates and records the best moments of her life.

Make it a celebration to forever be remembered with pageantry and splendor.

A Place for Holding Court

Dye Recipes

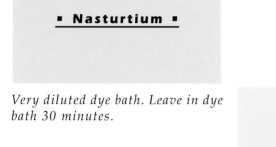

▪ Nasturtium ▪

Very diluted dye bath. Leave in dye bath 30 minutes.

.05 oz. Nasturtium (4 oz. mixed)

Used with Dining Chair Cover on page 49; Dressing Screen on page 48; Gift Bag on page 47; Wedding Album Photo Pages on page 54.

▪ Ice Mauve ▪

Diluted dye bath. Leave in dye bath 30 minutes.

.1 oz. Black (8 oz. mixed)

.2 oz. Lilac

Used with Dining Chair Cover on page 49; Place Setting on page 52; Table Drape on page 55; Wedding Album Photo Pages on page 54.

▪ Ice Orchid ▪

Very Diluted dye bath. Leave in dye bath 30 minutes.

.05 oz. Radiant Pink (4 oz. mixed)

.05 oz. Purple Vine (4 oz. mixed)

Used with Table Drape on page 55.

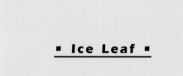

▪ Ice Leaf ▪

Very diluted dye bath. Leave in dye bath 30 minutes.

.05 oz. Leaf Green (4 oz. mixed)

.05 oz. Primrose (4 oz. mixed)

Used with Floral Umbrella on page 51; Place Setting on page 52.

▪ Tahiti Rose ▪

Diluted dye bath. Leave in dye bath 30 minutes.

.2 oz. Tahiti Rose

Used with Flower Girl Dress on page 56; Gloves & Hair Wreath on page 57; Table Drape on page 55.

Gift Bag

1 Remove drawstring on sachet bag. **2** Refer to General Dyeing Instructions on page 12 and Dye Recipes on page 46. Prepare dye bath. Randomly dye laces Nasturtium. Press all items while slightly damp. **3** Randomly adhere motifs and doilies to bag. Thread ribbon through eyelets at top of bag.

Supplies
(for one)

Fiber-reactive dye: (.05 oz.) Nasturtium

Lace doily: 4" round, White, Irish rose

Lace motifs: (3–4) assorted

Ribbon: (½ yd.) ½"-wide, Pale Yellow

Sachet bag: 4" x 5", White, eyelet

Dressing Screen

Supplies

Fiber-reactive dye: (.05 oz.) Nasturtium

Lace table runners: (6) 16" x 54", White, Tuscany

Paint: (64 oz.) White, satin finish; primer

Ribbon: (6 yds.) 1"-wide, Cream

Room divider form: 50" x 63½" x ¾", untreated wood

1 Refer to General Dyeing Instructions on page 12 and Dye Recipes on page 46. Prepare dye bath and dye table runners Nasturtium. Press while slightly damp. 2 Prime room divider screen. Let dry and sand. Paint room divider. Let dry and sand. Assemble room divider form, following manufacturer's instructions. 3 Sew length of ribbon to wrong side widths of each table runner top and bottom, turning ribbon under at ends to form casing. Insert dowel (provided with room divider form) through ribbon casing of two table runners, then insert dowel into one section of room divider slots. Insert a second dowel through ribbon casing at bottom edge of table runners, and insert dowel into bottom room divider slots. Repeat for each section.

Dining Chair Cover

Supplies

Fiber-reactive dyes: (.05 oz.) Nasturtium; (.1 oz.) Black; (.2 oz) Lilac

Linen napkin: 20", White, hemstitched

Linen towels: 28" x 44", White, cutwork; (2) 14" x 22", White, cutwork

1 Refer to General Dyeing Instructions on page 12 and Dye Recipes on page 46. Prepare dye baths. Dye towels Ice Mauve and napkin Nasturtium. Press while slightly damp. 2 Cut 28" x 44" towel in half, creating two 22" x 28" pieces. Use cutwork piece for front of chair cover and second piece for lining of chair cover. 3 Measure chair seat and add 3½" to each side and back. Cut chair and front lining pieces to these dimensions. Refer to Towel Placement Diagram below. At back edge, cut "L" shaped notches to accommodate chair back and round front corners as indicated by dashed lines on diagram. Place 14" x 22" towels at 45-degree angles over chair cover, meeting one corner of each at center of chair cover as shown. Sew over chair cover. Trim excess from 14" x 22" towels to match chair cover dimensions. Extra pieces can be pieced to chair cover as desired. 4 For chair cover ties, cut eight 1¼" x 8" strips from trimmed excess fabric. Fold strips with right sides together lengthwise. Sew one short end and long side taking ¼" seam. Turn right side out. 5 Pin ties to corners of chair cover front, matching raw edges. Pin front to lining, right sides together, aligning finished edge of front with finished edge of lining. Sew, taking ¼" – ½" seam allowance and leaving open entire finished edge of front and lining. Trim bulk from corners and clip fabric at inward corners to stitching. Turn right side out and press. 6 Insert napkin in-between front and lining, so about 2" of napkin hangs out from front.

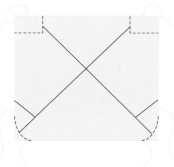

Towel Placement Diagram

Wedding Garter

1 Cut two 4¼" x 13" strips from drawn threadwork handkerchief, using finished edge for each strip. From remaining scrap, cut two 4¼" x 2½" strips, using finished edge for each strip. Cut one 4¼" x 13" and one 1½" x 13" strip from crocheted lace-trimmed handkerchief. **2** Overlap and sew each 4¼" x 13" drawn threadwork strip to a 4¼" x 2½" strip, using a narrow zigzag stitch, forming two 4¼" x 15" strips. Make certain 13" finished edge is aligned with 2½" finished edge and 4¼" finished edge is on top of 4¼" raw edge. **3** Overlap and sew each finished edge of 4¼" x 13" crochet lace-trimmed handkerchief onto remaining 4¼" raw edge of each 4¼" x 15" strip, using a narrow zigzag stitch and forming one long strip. **4** Press unfinished edge under 1" to wrong side of strip. Sew ⅜" from folded edge. Sew again ⅜" from first stitching, turning raw edge under while stitching, forming a

Supplies

Elastic: (½ yd.) ¼"-wide

Lace handkerchiefs: 13" square, White, drawn threadwork; 13" square, White, crocheted edge

Ribbon: (1 yd.) 4mm-wide, Pale Tahiti Rose, silk

casing for elastic. **5** Measure thigh for elastic length, cut elastic to measurement plus 1". Insert elastic through casing. Stitch elastic ends together, taking a ½" seam allowance, creating garter center. Work elastic seam into casing. **6** Refer to Gathered Rosebud on page 26. Fold and press 1½" x 13" strip in half lengthwise. Make rose with folded strip. Stitch rose to casing at garter center. Fold ribbon in half. Hold folded ribbon together and tie as one ribbon length into small bow. Tack bow near rose, knot ribbon ends.

Floral Umbrella

Supplies

Fiber-reactive dyes: (.05 oz. each) Leaf Green; Primrose

Floral oasis

Florist tape

Florist tubes (optional)

Fresh flowers

Lace umbrella: 12", White, crocheted edge

Sheet plastic

1 Refer to General Dyeing Instructions on page 12 and Dye Recipes on page 46. Prepare dye bath and dye umbrella Ice Leaf, using a plastic tub that umbrella will fit into when half opened. Wet umbrella. Dip half-opened umbrella into dye bath and swirl around so umbrella dyes evenly. Rinse with cold water. Shake out excess moisture from umbrella. Open umbrella fully to dry. 2 Stabilize open umbrella on work surface, inside up. Line inside of umbrella with plastic. Do not line outer crochet-trimmed edge. Size oasis and cut to fit center of umbrella. Wet oasis, then place in umbrella. Use umbrella spokes and florist tape to secure oasis. Fill with fresh flowers. For a longer lasting arrangement, place flowers in individual water-filled tubes before inserting into oasis.

Place Setting

Supplies (for one)

Fabric marker: Pink

Fiber-reactive dyes: (.05 oz. each) Leaf Green;
  Primrose; (.1 oz.) Black; (.2 oz) Lilac

Florist tape

Florist wire: (4½")

Napkin: 18" square, White with Cluny lace trim

Lace doilies: 2", White, Battenburg, heart; 4",
  White, Reticella, round; 6" White, Irish rose,
  round; 8" White, Tuscany, round

Lace trim: (1 yd.) 1¼"-wide, White, Cluny

Placecard

Ribbon: (½ yd.) 1½"-wide, White

Rubber stamp: rose

1 Refer to General Dyeing Instructions on page 12 and Dye Recipes on page 46. Prepare dye baths. Dye trim and 2" doily Ice Leaf and napkin Ice Mauve. Press all items while slightly damp. 2 For doily charger, steam press trim so that it curves, matching the outer edge of 8" doily and overlapping 1½" on ends. On wrong side of doily, sew straight edge of lace to inner scalloped edge, using a narrow zigzag stitch. Press. 3 Refer to Doily Rosette on page 25. Lightly color edges of 6" doily with fabric marker. Mist with water and press dry. Fold doily in half, right sides out. Bend a small loop at one end of florist wire. Place loop at right edge of doily near bottom fold. Sew wire to doily through loop. Finish rosette. Wrap thread several times around doily, secure thread. Cut center from 4" and 2" doilies, creating ¾"-wide center openings. Gather-stitch ¼" from cut edge. Slip wired rosebud through center of 4" doily. Pull gather thread as tightly as possible so doily gathers around rosebud. Wrap thread several times around rosebud and knot. Shape doily petals. Repeat with 2" doily. Wrap florist tape around wire beginning just below 2" doily. 4 Fold and pleat napkin, wrap pleats snugly with ribbon and tie into a bow. Curl loose end of wire and slip rose through napkin pleats. 5 Adhere lace scraps to placecard as desired. Stamp placecard with rubber stamp and color as desired.

Wedding Album Photo Pages

Supplies (for two)

Album pages: (2)

Crocheted flowers: (2) 2", White

Fiber-reactive dyes: (.1 oz.)
    Black; (.2 oz. each) Lilac;
    Nasturtium

Lace doily: 4" round, White

Lace trims: (1 yd. each)
    4"-wide White, Cluny;
    1¼"-wide, White, Cluny;
    ¼"-wide, White, tatted;
    ½"-wide, White, tatted

Silk ribbon: (1 yd.) 4 mm-wide;
    Pale Yellow

1 Refer to General Dyeing Instructions on page 12 and Dye Recipes on page 46. Wet all laces. Use towel to blot excess water. Prepare dye baths. Dye doily and flowers Nasturtium and all trims Ice Mauve. Press all items while slightly damp. **2** On one album page, mark and cut out a 5" x 7" opening in center. Adhere 1¼" trim to sides of opening. Adhere 4" trim to bottom edge of page, trimming lace flush to page at edges. Cut doily in half. Adhere to center top of page with raw edge down and parallel to opening. Adhere ¼" and ½" trims to top edge of opening, covering raw edge of doily. Tie two small bows with ribbon and trim tails. Adhere bows over 1¼" trim at top corners of opening. **3** On second album page, cut large oval shape, making certain bottom of oval has a straight edge. Steam press ½" and 1¼" trims to curve, matching oval edge. Adhere 1¼" trim to oval, facing scallops inward. Adhere 4" trim diagonally across top, outer edge of page and across bottom flat edge of oval. Adhere ½" trim to oval, facing scallops outward and covering flat edge of 4" trim. Tie a small bow with ribbon and trim tails. Adhere to bottom center of oval. Adhere a flower to either side of bow.

Table Drape

Supplies (for one)

Fiber-reactive dyes: (.05 oz. each) Radiant Pink; Purple Vine; (.1 oz.) Black; (.2 oz. each) Lilac; Tahiti Rose

Lace tablecloths: 72" round, White, crochet; 54" square, White, hemstitched

Lace table toppers: (2) 36" square, White, filet crochet

1 Refer to General Dyeing Instructions on page 12 and Dye Recipes on page 46. Prepare dye baths. Dye 54" tablecloth Tahiti Rose, 72" tablecloth Ice Orchid, and one table topper Ice Mauve. Press all items while slightly damp. 2 Refer to Fabric Stamping on page 20. Stamp 54" tablecloth as desired. 3 Layer pieces on table with 72" tablecloth as bottom layer, 54" tablecloth as middle, and table toppers offset together as top.

Flower Girl Dress

1 Refer to General Dyeing Instructions on page 12 and Dye Recipes on page 46. Prepare dye bath and dye placemats, flowers, and napkins Tahiti Rose. Press while slightly damp. **2** Cut bodice front and back from linen, following pattern instructions. Cut 1½"-wide bias binding from linen to finish neck edge and bodice. **3** Cut one placemat in half lengthwise. Overlap and pin placemat halves to bodice front so they are angled slightly and meet at center of drop waist seam. Center and pin a piece of 4" trim to bodice center front just below neckline. Trim lace so scalloped edge of placemats overlap lace ¼". Stitch 4" trim in place. Pin 1¼" trim underneath scalloped edges of placemats. Stitch placemats and lace trim to bodice front, following scalloped shape of placemats. Sew bodice front to back at shoulders. **4** Cut second placemat into two pieces that measure 5" wide, with each having a finished edge, for collar. Gather-stich two rows along cut edge of each collar. Pull gathers to fit each neck edge, front to back. Pin in place. Finish neck edge and bodice, with bias binding. **5** Cut a 4" wide strip from each napkin and set aside. To make the skirt, overlap and stitch remaining napkin portions together. Pin cut edge of strips to cut edge of skirt (strips are not stitched together). Gather-stitch two rows along cut edges of skirt. Pull gathers to fit bodice drop waist seam. Pin skirt to bodice, right sides together. Sew seam. Trim seam to ¼" and overcast. Edge-stitch skirt seam to bodice close to seam. **6** Sew flowers to bodice center front.

Supplies

Crocheted flowers: (5) 2", White

Dress pattern: for drop-waisted, sleeveless dress with gathered skirt

Fiber-reactive dye: (.2 oz) Tahiti Rose

Lace trim: (¼ yd.) 4"-wide, White, Cluny; (1 yd.) 1¼"-wide, White, Cluny

Linen: (amount according to pattern) 44"-wide, White

Napkins: (4) 18", White, shadow embroidery

Placemats: (2) 14" x 20", White, shadow embroidery

Gloves & Hair Wreath

Supplies

Crocheted flowers: (4) 3",
White; (2) 2", White

Fiber-reactive dye: (.2 oz) Tahiti
Rose

Lace flowers: (3) 5" x 4", White,
Belgian

Lace gloves: White

Lace trim: (¼ yd.) 4"-wide,
White, Cluny

Ribbon: (1 yd.) 1"-wide, White

Ribbon flowers: (14) 1¼", White,
rayon; (17) 1", White, rayon

Wreath form: 5½" ring, White or
as desired

1 Refer to General Dyeing Instructions on page 12 and Dye Recipes on page 46. Do not preshrink 3" flowers. Prepare dye bath and dye gloves, 2" flowers, ribbon flowers, and lace flowers Tahiti Rose. Leave nine 1¼" ribbon flowers in the dye bath for a full hour. Press all items but ribbon flowers while slightly damp. **2** On each glove, hand-stitch one 3" flower to center front at wrist. Hand-stitch one 2" flower over center of 3" flower. **3** Wrap wreath form with ribbon. Ribbon overlap will be center back. Mark center back and center front of ring. Cut an evenly spaced 15" length from 4" trim. Gather-stitch across cut ends, pull gathers tight and knot thread. Gather-stitch straight edge of trim and pull gathers so that lace measures 7". Knot thread. Measure and mark 3½" from center back of ring on each side. Hand-stitch gathered edge of trim to ring between marks. Tack or adhere ribbon and lace flowers to ring as desired.

Nothing is quite as comfortable or as comforting as a room dressed in garden flowers and lace. Such a room tells of time spent quietly to replenish the body, soul, and mind.

It is filled with the tiny luxuries of bath salts tied in hand-dyed lace, creamy soap wrapped in misty blue cotton, lightly scented water with a hundred million bubbles, and white clouds of perfumed lavender or peach.

A place where bathing and pampering exist solely to soothe the mind and body, revive the senses, and invigorate the soul.

Dye Recipes

▪ Sea Green ▪

Leave in dye bath 30 to 60 minutes, depending on color depth desired.

.2 oz. Sea Green

Used with Boutique Tissue Box on page 66; Lace-wrapped Candleholder on page 63; Lucite Box on page 66; Sea Green Guest Towel on page 70; Soap Wraps on page 64.

▪ Riviera Blue ▪

Diluted dye bath. Leave in dye bath 30 minutes, depending on color depth desired.

.1 oz. Riviera Blue (8 oz. mixed)

Used with Blue Guest Towel on page 68; Candlestick Liner on page 65.

Butterfly Dress

Supplies

Baby rickrack: (3 yd.) ⅛"-wide, Yellow

Button: ¾", Yellow/White, sunflower

Fabric: (amount according to pattern) 44"-wide, Blue/White, cotton, cloud pattern; (½ yd.) 44"-wide Pale Green print

Jumper pattern: simple

Lace collar: 2½"-wide, White, child size, crocheted

Lace motifs: (6) 4" x 3", White, butterfly, Belgian

1 Cut dress from Blue/White fabric, using pattern. Cut 1½"-wide bias binding from Pale Green print fabric to finish neck edge, armholes and hem. Sew dress, following pattern instructions. Finish neck edge, armholes and hem with bias binding. **2** Pin collar to front neck edge and shoulders. Steam press to fit, as necessary. Sew collar to neck edge and shoulders at binding seam using a narrow zigzag stitch. Sew baby rickrack to armholes and hem at binding seams. **3** Pin and sew butterflies onto dress front near hemmed edge as desired. **4** Sew button to neck edge at center front.

Doily Sachet

Supplies
(for one)

Crystal or glass rock: Light Blue, Mint, or Turquoise

Fabric: 6" or 8"-diameter circle, Blue, Mint, or Turquoise, cotton

Lace Doily: 5" or 6", White, round with Cluny edge

Potpourri

Ribbon: (12") 9 mm-wide, Aqua, Light Blue, or Mint

1 Fold fabric circle in half, wrong sides together. Sew along curved edge with zigzag stich, leaving a small opening. Stuff with potpourri through opening. Sew opening closed. **2** Fold doily over potpourri-filled fabric. Pin and sew together at outer edges. **3** Cut ribbon in half. Fold ribbons together as one and tie into small bow. Sew bow to doily center, about 1" from fold, sewing through all layers. Sew crystal over bow center, stitching through all layers of sachet.

Lace-wrapped Candleholder

Supplies

Candleholder: 2½" x 3½", frosted with colored candle

Fiber-reactive dye: (.2 oz) Sea Green

Lace trim: (12") 3"-wide, White, crochet

Ribbon: (15") ½"-wide, Light Turquoise, grosgrain

1 Refer to General Dyeing Instructions on page 12 and Dye Recipes on page 60. Prepare dye baths. Dye trim Sea Green. Press while slightly damp. **2** Cut trim to circumference of candleholder plus 1". Apply a thin layer of tacky glue to wrong side of trim. Wrap trim snugly around candleholder, placing trim about ½" from top edge and overlapping ends. **3** Apply a thin layer of tacky glue to wrong side of ribbon. Apply to center of ribbon only. Wrap ribbon snugly around candleholder so that ends meet at the center of one lace scallop. Let dry. Tie ends into a small bow. Trim ends.

Supplies
(for two)

Bar soap: (2)

Fabric ink pad: Light Blue

Fiber-reactive dye: (.2 oz) Sea Green

Handkerchief: (2) 12" or 13", White, square with crocheted lace trim

Ribbon: (18" for each) ⅝"-wide, French Blue, grosgrain

Rubber stamp

1 Refer to General Dyeing Instructions on page 12 and Dye Recipes on page 60. Prepare dye bath and dye one handkerchief Sea Green. Press while slightly damp. **2** Refer to Fabric Stamping on page 20. Stamp top center of each corner of White handkerchief and color as desired. Press to heat set. **3** Place soap bar on center wrong side of each handkerchief. Fold edges of handkerchief evenly up around soap. Tie ribbon into bow around gathered end of handkerchiefs.

Supplies

Lace doily: 6", White, reticella

Beads: (about 15), Cobalt Blue, small, glass; (about 14) 11/0, Light Blue, seed

Candleholder: 5" tall, glass, for tapered candles.

Fabric stiffener: 4 oz.

Fiber-reactive dye: (.1 oz.) Riviera Blue

1 Refer to General Dyeing Instructions on page 12 and Dye Recipes on page 60. Prepare dye bath and dye doily Riviera Blue. Press while slightly damp. **2** Sew one or two different glass beads to every other doily point as desired.

3 Dip beaded doily in fabric stiffener, following manufacturer's instructions. Place doily center in candleholder, insert candle, and shape extending doily edges. Let dry. Fabric stiffener may adhere doily to candlestick.

Lucite Box

Supplies
(for one)

Fabric stiffener

Fiber-reactive dyes: (.2 oz)
Sea Green

Glass paint: Clear Frost

Lace doilies: 4", White, tatted,
heart; 4", White, round

Lace trim: (⅝ yd.) 4"-wide,
White

Lucite box: 4" x 5" or 4" x 7"

Ribbon: (18") ½"-wide, Aqua,
grosgrain

1 Refer to General Dyeing Instructions on page 12 and Dye Recipes on page 60. Prepare dye baths. Dye doilies and trim Sea Green. Press while slightly damp. **2** Remove lid from box. Sponge glass paint on top outside, excluding lid edges. Let dry. **3** Refer to Decoupage with Fabrics & Laces on page 18. Decoupage trim to sides of box on bottom half, centering an inner lace scallop on one box side. Overlap lace trim at back about 2". **4** On box lid, center and decoupage one 4" doily. Gather-stitch 1"-diameter circle in the center of second 4" doily. Dip gathered doily into fabric stiffener and shape. Let dry. Adhere stiffened doily to box top. **5** Decoupage grosgrain ribbon to box bottom edges. Overlap ribbon about ¼" at back.

Boutique Tissue Box

1 Refer to General Dyeing Instructions on page 12 and Dye Recipes on page 60. Prepare dye bath and dye collar inserts Sea Green. Press while slightly damp. **2** Paint inside and outside of tissue box Sky Blue. Let dry. Apply second coat on box inside. Lightly sand in-between coats. **3** Pour a small amount of the remaining paint shades onto paint palette. Sponge paint outside of tissue box, working with one paint shade at a time. Let dry. Lightly sand, then seal with acrylic varnish. **4** Refer to Decoupage with Fabrics & Laces on page 18. Decoupage collar inserts to tissue box as desired. Let dry. **5** Adhere ribbon around top edge of box and tie into bow at front. Knot ribbon ends and trim close to knots. Adhere knots off to side of bow. Hand-stitch beads to bow center

Supplies

Acrylic paint: Aqua, Sky Blue,
Leaf Green, Periwinkle

Acrylic varnish

Beads: Cobalt Blue, small

Fiber-reactive dye: (.2 oz) Sea
Green

Lace collar insert: (2) 9" x 7",
White, Belgian

Ribbon: (1 yd.) 1½"-wide,
Blue/Gold cross-dyed

Tissue box: 5" x 6", Natural,
wood

Heart-stamped Guest Towel

Supplies

Fabric ink pads: Sky Blue; Mint Green; Spring Green

Fabric markers: Aqua; Lime; Periwinkle

Lace trim: (18") 3"-wide, White, crocheted

Linen towel: 14" x 22", White, hemstitched

Rubber stamps: heart silhouette; pansy; small bird

Ruler: decorative-edged

1 Draw a 10" x 10" grid pattern on blank paper with 2"-wide sections. Darken grids with marker. Center grid underneath towel, beginning at upper edge of hem. **2** Refer to Fabric Stamping on page 20. Ink heart stamp with Sky Blue fabric ink pad. Stamp heart in the center grid nearest upper hem edge. Continue to ink and stamp heart, skipping every other grid space, as in a checkerboard. Ink pansy, stamp with Sky Blue fabric ink pad. Stamp pansy design in open grid spaces. Ink small bird stamp and randomly stamp among hearts and pansies. **3** Use scrubber brush to very lightly swirl color around heart, pansies, and birds with Mint Green and Spring Green ink. **4** Detail each design with Aqua, Lime, and Periwinkle fabric markers as desired. Heat set. **5** Trace decorative edge of ruler onto hemmed towel edge with Periwinkle marker.

Blue Guest Towel

Supplies

Fabric ink pad: Spring Green

Fabric markers: fine-tipped Aqua; Emerald; Leaf Green; Spring Green; Sky Mist; Periwinkle

Fiber-reactive dye: (.1 oz.) Riviera Blue

Linen towel: 28" x 44", White with filet crocheted edge

Rubber stamp: flower

1 Refer to General Dyeing Instructions on page 12 and Dye Recipes on page 60. Prepare dye bath and dye towel a light shade of Riviera Blue. Press while slightly damp. **2** Ink stamp with Spring Green fabric ink pad. Center and stamp flower on left side of towel above lace trimmed edge. Repeat, centering flower on right side of towel and inverting image for a mirror effect. Heat set. **3** Darken design with Spring Green fabric marker. Highlight design with Emerald and Sky Mist fabric markers. Add detail to stems with Leaf Green fabric marker. Add scalloped detail to leaves along one edge with Aqua fabric marker. Add scalloped detail to petals and buds with Periwinkle fabric marker. Heat set.

Sea Green Guest Towel

Supplies

Fiber-reactive dye: (.2 oz) Sea Green

Lace trim: (18") 3"-wide, crocheted

Linen towel: 14" x 22", White with shadow embroidery

Ribbon: (18") 7 mm-wide, Light Blue

1 Refer to General Dyeing Instructions on page 12 and Dye Recipes on page 60. Prepare dye bath and dye towel and trim Sea Green. Dye towel a light shade and lace a dark shade. Press while slightly damp. **2** Weave ribbon through straight edge of trim. Sew trim to bottom edge of guest towel with narrow zigzag stitch. Hem cut ends of trim even with towel at sides.

Embroidered Guest Towel

1 Refer to Fabric Paints on page 19. Pour paints onto palette. Lightly mist with water to slightly thin paints. Slightly mix paints together for an Ice Blue shade. Paint some of towel above lace trim, leaving some portions of towel white, using paintbrush and broad strokes. Let dry. Heat set. Wash towel in warm, soapy water to soften paint. Press while slightly damp. **2** Transfer Bouquet Pattern and Border Pattern on page 72 to towel, using erasable fabric marker or pencil and taping pattern to a well lit window or other light source. Refer to Embroidery Stitch Guide, Bouquet Stitch Diagram, and Border Stitch Diagram on page 72, and Embellishments on pages 24–27. Embroider with three strands of floss for each stitch. **3** Embroider hemstitched portion of guest towel with buttonhole stitch and Powder Blue floss. **4** Tie ribbon around flower stems, then tie ribbon into a small bow. Trim ribbon ends short and tie knots at ends.

Supplies

Embroidery floss: Aqua; Ice Blue; Powder Blue; Mint Green

Fabric paints: Pearl Blue; Pearl White

Linen towel; 14" x 22", White with filet crochet edge

Paintbrush: 1"-wide, flat

Ribbon: (9") 4 mm-wide, Blue, silk

Embroidery Stitch Guide

Item	Floss	Stitch
Stems	Mint Green	Outline Stitch
Flower Petals	Ice Blue, Powder Blue	Bullion Lazy Daisy
Flower Centers	Ice Blue, Powder Blue	Colonial Knot
Leaves	Aqua	Bullion Lazy Daisy

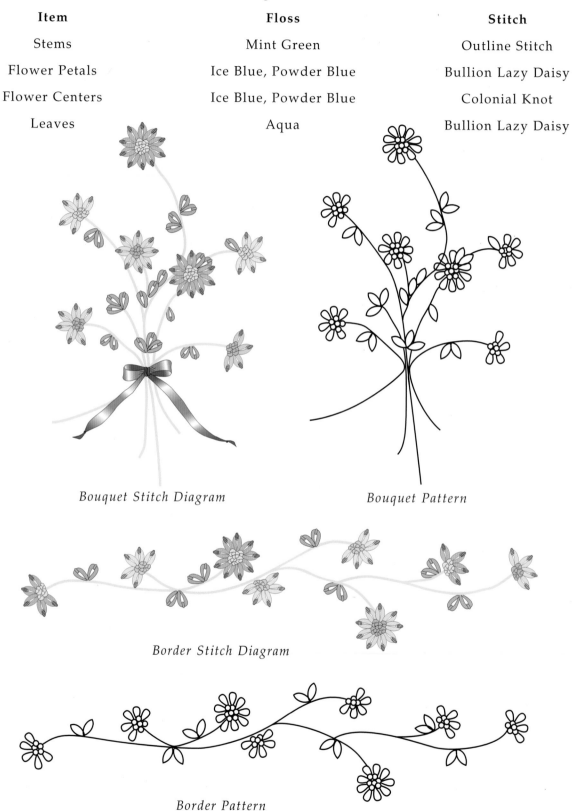

Bouquet Stitch Diagram

Bouquet Pattern

Border Stitch Diagram

Border Pattern

Supplies

Lace table runners: (2) 16" x 90",
White, filet crochet

1 Fold one end of each table runner under 22". Sew 1" from fold and again 4" from fold, forming pocket. **2** Hang on shower curtain rod as desired.

Embroidered Napkin

Supplies

Embroidery floss: (one skein)
  Blue variegated

Linen napkin: 6", White, hemstitched

1 Transfer Napkin Pattern on page 75 to napkin center, using a erasable fabric marker or pencil and taping pattern to a well lit window or other light source. **2** Refer to Embroidery Stitch Guide and Napkin Stitch Diagram on page 75, and Embellishments on pages 24–27. Embroider with three strands of floss for each stitch.

Napkin Pattern

Napkin Stitch Diagram

Embroidery Stitch Guide

Item	Floss	Stitch
Where indicated by "X"	Blue Variegated	Cross-stitch
Flower Petals	Blue Variegated	Lazy Daisy
Flower Centers	Blue Variegated	Colonial Knot

A Place for Good Company

What could be more wonderful than creating a place for good company to stay for awhile. Somewhere that is welcoming, comfortable, and calming. Somewhere private that can be casually enjoyed by family or friends. A temporary room of their own that has an approachable, yet sophisticated style. A room filled with enchantment and a symphony of texture and color. A place to quietly read, share long-kept secrets, or dream under coverlets of lace.

Dye Recipes

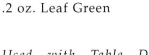

Tree Moss

.2 oz. Koala Brown

.2 oz. Leaf Green

Used with Table Drape on page 86.

Chocolate

.1 oz. Black (8 oz. mixed)

.2 oz. Leaf Green

.4 oz. Tartan Green

.2 oz. Mexican Red

Used with Bed Throw on page 83; Stacking Box on page 84; Straw Hat on page 90; Sweater Vest on page 92.

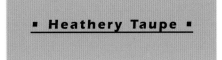

Heathery Taupe

.05 oz. Black (4 oz. mixed)

.4 oz. Café au Lait

.05 oz. Ultraviolet (4 oz. mixed)

Used with Bed Skirt & Pillow-cases on page 88; Coverlet on page 80; Straw Hat on page 90.

Plum

.2 oz. Black

.2 oz. Koala Brown

.6 oz. Ultraviolet

Used with Sweater Vest on page 92; Table Drape on page 86; Window Valance on page 85.

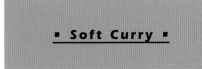

Soft Curry

.2 oz. Koala Brown

.05 oz. Nasturtium (4 oz. mixed)

.6 oz. Sahara Sun

Used with Coverlet on page 80.

Rusted

.2 oz. Café au Lait

.2 oz. Bronze Rose

Used with Picture Frame on page 87; Throw Pillows on page 79; Sachet Ball on page 91.

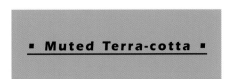

Muted Terra-cotta

.2 oz. Café au Lait

.4 oz. Koala Brown

Used with Throw Pillows on page 79; Table Drape on page 86; Window Valance on page 85.

Throw Pillow

Supplies (for one)

Broadcloth: (⅓ yd.) 44"-wide, Olive or Dusty Rose

Fiber-reactive dyes: (.2 oz) Bronze Rose;
   (.4 oz. each) Koala Brown; Café au Lait;

Grosgrain ribbon: (1 yd.) ⅜"-wide, Khaki or Olive

Polyester stuffing: (12 oz.)

Ribbon flowers: (10) 1¼", Ivory, rayon

Table runner: 16" x 54", Beige, Tuscany

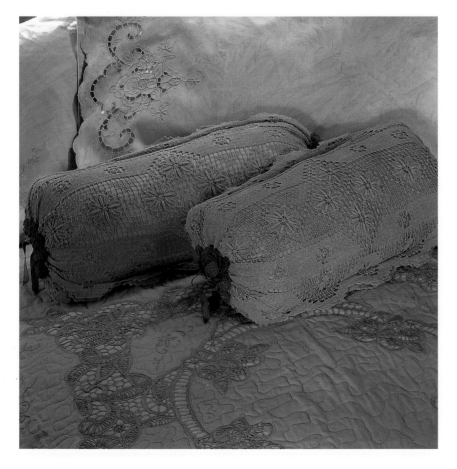

1 Refer to General Dyeing Instructions on page 12 and Dye Recipes on page 78. Prepare dye baths. Dye table runner Muted Terra-cotta and flowers Rusted. Press table runner while slightly damp. Let flowers dry. **2** To make pillow, fold and pin width ends of table runner to center, overlapping about 3" (this will be center back of pillow). Make certain scalloped shapes line up lengthwise with each other. Topstitch front to back, placing stitches 1¼" in from top and bottom scalloped edges of folded runner. Gather-stitch across runner at folded edges. Pull and knot thread. **3** Refer to Pillow Forms on page 22. Make pillow form. Insert form into pillow through back at overlap. **4** Cut ribbon in half. Tie each piece into a 3"-wide bow. Hand-stitch a bow and five flowers to each gathered end of pillow.

Coverlet

Supplies

▪ all sizes ▪

Batting: to fit size, heirloom cotton (optional)

Fiber-reactive dyes: (.05 oz. each) Black; Nasturtium; Ultraviolet; (.2 oz) Koala Brown; (.4 oz.) Café au Lait; (.6 oz.) Sahara Sun

Additional Supplies

▪ twin-size coverlet ▪

Sheets: (2) full-size, Rose Beige or Dusty Rose; or, (5½ yds.) 90"-wide, muslin or broadcloth

Tablecloth: 72" x 90" with 4" Battenburg lace edge

▪ full-size coverlet ▪

Sheets: (2) queen-size, Rose Beige or Dusty Rose; or, (8 yds.) 44"-wide, muslin or broadcloth

Tablecloth: 72" x 90" with 4" Battenburg lace edge

Table runners: (2) 16" x 45" with 4" Battenburg lace edge

▪ queen-size coverlet ▪

Sheets: (2) king-size Rose Beige or Dusty Rose; or, (9 yds.) 44"-wide, muslin or broadcloth

Tablecloth: 72" x 108" with 4" Battenburg lace edge

Table runners: (4) 16" x 54" with 4" Battenburg lace edge

▪ king-size coverlet ▪

Sheets: (3) queen-size, Rose Beige or Dusty Rose; or, (9 yds.) 44"-wide, muslin or broadcloth

Tablecloth: 72" x 108" with 4" Battenburg lace edge

Table toppers: (2) 54" square with 4" Battenburg lace edge

1 Refer to General Dyeing Instructions on page 12 and Dye Recipes on page 78. Prepare dye baths. Dye all selected fabrics and laces Soft Curry. (Do not dye sheets.) Overdye tablecloth Heathery Taupe. Press while slightly damp. **2** Two equal-sized pieces will be used for the coverlet lining and backing. Tablecloth is used for coverlet top. Piece fabric lengthwise for lining and backing, if necessary and sew. Make certain that lining and backing fabrics extend 4" beyond coverlet top on all sides. **3** Machine-quilt coverlet top, lining, batting, and backing together. **4** To finish coverlet edge, trim backing and batting flush with outer edge of lace trim on top edge only. Trim lining 1¼" longer than edge of lace, batting, and backing on top edge. Trim backing and batting flush with inner edge of lace trim on remaining three edges. Trim lining 1¼" longer than edges of batting and backing on remaining three sides. Fold lining edge over batting and backing edges to underside of coverlet. Turn raw edge of lining under and hand-hem all sides in place.

For Full-size Coverlet

Refer to Overlapping Laces on page 22. Cut each table runner in half lengthwise. Overlap finished tablecloth edge onto cut edge of table runners, positioning table runners as shown in diagram at right. Sew in place with a narrow zigzag stitch. Trim excess lace from underside, if necessary.

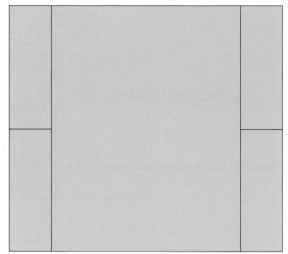

Full-sized Coverlet Diagram

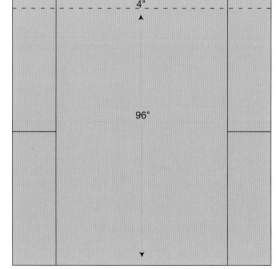

Queen-sized Coverlet Diagram

For Queen-size Coverlet

Refer to Overlapping Laces on page 22. Trim tablecloth to 72" x 100". Mark in 4" lengthwise along cut edge. Trim table runners to 12" x 54". Overlap table runners at center, beginning at 4" mark, to fit a 96" length of tablecloth as shown in diagram to left. Overlap finished tablecloth edge onto cut edge of table runners as shown in diagram at left. Sew in place with a narrow zigzag stitch. Trim excess lace from underside, if necessary.

For King-size Coverlet

Refer to Overlapping Laces on page 22. Trim tablecloth as instructed for Queen-sized Coverlet. Trim 54" square table toppers, creating four pieces measuring 18" x 54", and so that each piece has three lace-trimmed edges. Overlap finished edge of uncut tablecloth onto cut edge of each 18" x 54" table topper pieces as shown in diagram at right. Sew in place with a narrow zigzag stitch. Trim excess lace from underside, if necessary.

King-sized Coverlet Diagram

Bed Throw

Supplies

▪ one size fits all ▪

Fiber-reactive dyes: (.1 oz.)
 Black; (.2 oz. each) Leaf
 Green; Mexican Red;
 (.4 oz.) Tartan Green

Flannel: (1¼" yds.) 54"-wide,
 plaid

Lace table topper: 54" square,
 Beige, cotton knit

1 Refer to General Dyeing Instructions on page 12 and Dye Recipes on page 78. Prepare dye bath and dye table topper Chocolate. Press while slightly damp. (If topper stretches out of shape at the corners, it will steam back into shape when the flannel backing is added.) **2** Trim flannel to a 44" square. Narrowly hem edges. **3** Prepare a large work surface, such as a carpeted floor, and have a steam iron ready. Place flannel, right side up, onto work surface.

Place table topper, right side up, onto flannel. Pin table topper to flannel, beginning at center of topper and working outward to edge centers. Allow scalloped lace edge to remain unbacked. Fit and pin table topper corners evenly to flannel corners, working one corner at a time. Use iron to steam topper into shape and fit to flannel. **4** Sew topper to flannel at outer edges and along knitted design lines to maintain shape of table topper. Press.

Stacking Box

1 Refer to General Dyeing Instructions on page 12 and Dye Recipes on page 78. Prepare dye bath and dye all selected laces Chocolate. Press while slightly damp. For an alternative method, paint lace with dark brown acrylic paint. **2** Place small amount of each paint shade on paint pallet. Mix paints slightly. Paint inside and outside of each box section. Let dry. Paint shade will be very dark brown, almost black. **3** Refer to Decoupage with Fabric & Laces on page 18. Decoupage all laces to box sections as desired. Let dry. **4** Using paintbrush, apply thin coat of decoupage medium over outside of box sections and laces. Let dry. Apply second coat of decoupage medium.

Supplies

Acrylic decorator glaze: Black; Bark Brown; Russet Brown; Deep Purple

Decoupage medium: antique finish

Fiber-reactive dyes: (.1 oz.) Black; (.2 oz. each) Leaf Green; Mexican Red; (.4 oz.) Tartan Green

Lace doily: 4", Beige, knitted

Lace trims: (1 yd.) 1¼"-wide, Cluny; (½ yd.) 3"-wide, crocheted; (1½ yd.) ¼"-wide, tatted

Papier maché box: 4¾" x 8" cylinder with three stacking sections and lid

Window Valance

Supplies
(for one small window)

Fiber-reactive dyes: (.2 oz) Café au Lait; (.4 oz.) Koala Brown

Lace table topper: 54" round, Tuscany

1 Refer to General Dyeing Instructions on page 12 and Dye Recipes on page 78. Prepare dye bath and dye table topper Muted Terra-cotta. Press while slightly damp. **2** Cut topper in half. Fold and press cut edges under 4" to wrong side of lace. Sew 1" from pressed edge. Turn cut edge under ½" and sew in place, forming a 2½"-wide rod pocket. Hang as desired.

Table Drape

1 Refer to General Dyeing Instructions on page 12 and Dye Recipes on page 78. Prepare dye baths. Dye tablecloth Muted Terra-cotta, table topper Plum, and table runner Tree Moss. Press all pieces while slightly damp. **2** Layer and drape pieces onto round table. Tablecloth is bottom layer. Add table topper and finish with table runner.

Supplies

Fiber-reactive dyes: (.2 oz. each)
   Black; Café au Lait; Leaf
   Green; (.6 oz.) Ultraviolet;
   (.8 oz.) Koala Brown

Lace table runner: 16" x 36",
   Beige, drawn threadwork
   with tatted lace edge

Lace table topper: 54" square,
   Beige, Tuscany

Tablecloth: 72" round, Beige
   with filet crocheted edge

Picture Frame

1 Refer to General Dyeing Instructions on page 12 and Dye Recipes on page 78. Prepare dye bath and dye all selected laces Rusted. Press while slightly damp. For an alternative method, paint lace with rust acrylic paint. **2** Place small amount of Black and Ivy Green paint on paint palette. Mix paints slightly. Paint outside of frame form, allowing paint to streak. Let dry. Paint will be a unique shade of Olive Green. **3** Place small amount of remaining paint shades onto palette. Do not mix paints. Lightly sponge paints onto all selected laces so paint soaks in and they take on additional dimension. Let dry. **4** Refer to Decoupage with Fabric & Laces on page 18. Cut 6" doily in half. Decoupage laces to frame as desired.

Supplies

Acrylic decorator glazes: Black; Bronze; Russet Brown; Copper; New Leaf Gold; Ivy Green

Decoupage medium: antique finish

Fiber-reactive dyes: (.2 oz. each) Café au Lait; Bronze Rose

Frame: 8" x 10" papier maché

Lace doilies; 6", Beige, with Cluny lace edge; (2) 4", Beige, Cluny

Lace motifs: Rose; (2) small leaf; (2) medium leaf

Lace trim: ¼"-wide, White, tatted

Bed Skirt & Pillowcases

Supplies

▪ all sizes ▪

Fiber-reactive dyes: (.05 oz.
each) Black; Ultraviolet;
(.4 oz.) Café au Lait

Pillowcases: White, cutwork

Additional Supplies

▪ twin-size bed skirt ▪

Broadcloth: (2¼ yds.) 44"-wide

Table runners: (3) 16" x 72"

▪ full-size bed skirt ▪

Broadcloth: (4⅜ yds.) 44"-wide

Table runners: (2) 16" x 72";
(2) 16" x 45"

▪ queen-size bed skirt ▪

Broadcloth: (4⅝ yds.) 44"-wide

Table runners: (2) 16" x 72";
(2) 16" x 45"

▪ king-size bed skirt ▪

Broadcloth: (2⅜ yds.) 90"-wide
or (4⅝ yds.) 44"-wide

Table runners: (4) 16" x 72"

1 Refer to General Dyeing Instructions on page 12 and Dye Recipes on page 78. Prepare dye bath and dye all selected fabrics and laces Heathery Taupe. Press while slightly damp. **2** Refer to Dimensions below. Trim or piece broadcloth to appropriate size. Finish one width-edge with a doubled 1" hem. At opposite edge, round corners slightly, using fabric scissors. **3** Working lengthwise and beginning at hemmed edge, pin edge of one table runner to one lengthwise edge of broadcloth. Refer to appropriate Diagram at left for placement. Pin edge of second table runner lengthwise to opposite edge of broadcloth. Pin remaining table runners to broadcloth as indicated. Table runners pinned to edge of broadcloth widthwise will extend over the table runners pinned to edges lengthwise at and around corners. **4** Sew table runners to broadcloth, taking a ¼" seam allowance. Overcast seam and press towards broadcloth. Top-stitch seam.

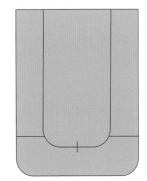

Twin-size Bed Skirt Diagram

Full-size Bed Skirt Diagram

Queen-size Bed Skirt Diagram

Dimensions:
For Twin-size Bed Skirt

Trim broadcloth to 39" x 77". Mark center of unfinished, rounded edge of broadcloth. Mark center of third table runner along one length. Center and pin mark on table runner to mark on broadcloth.

For Full-size Bed Skirt

Piece broadcloth vertically to 54" x 77".

For Queen-size Bed Skirt

Piece broadcloth vertically to 60" x 82".

For King-size Bed Skirt

Piece broadcloth vertically to 76" x 82".

King-size Bed Skirt Diagram

Straw Hat

Supplies

Button: ⅝", copper or wood

Cording: (½ yd.) narrow, Red-brown

Crocheted flowers: (4) 3" round, Beige

Fiber-reactive dyes: (.05 oz.) Ultraviolet; (.15 oz.) Black; (.2 oz. each) Koala Brown; Leaf Green; Mexican Red; (.4 oz. each) Café au Lait; Tartan Green

Lace doily: 6" round, Beige, knitted

Lace trim: (1 yd.) 4"-wide, Beige, filet crocheted

Straw hat

1 Refer to General Dyeing Instructions on page 12 and Dye Recipes on page 78. Prepare dye baths. Dye trim and flowers Heathery Taupe and doily Chocolate. Let flowers dry. Press laces while slightly damp. **2** Hem cut ends of trim. Snugly wrap trim around hat crown, overlapping at center back so trim ends drape onto brim. Hand-tack trim to crown with matching thread. **3** Gather center of doily. Hand-stitch to hat where trim overlaps. Gather centers of three flowers. Hand-stitch to center of doily. Hand-stitch remaining flower to hat crown to the right of doily flower. Hand-stitch a button to flower center. Make a six-looped bow from cording. Knot cording ends. Drape and tack to lace, close to flowers.

Sachet Ball

Supplies (for one)

Fiber-reactive dyes: (.2 oz. each) Café au Lait; Bronze Rose

Grosgrain ribbon: (⅓ yd.) ⅜"-wide, Natural

Lace doily: 10" round, Beige, knitted or Cluny

Potpourri

Ribbon flower: 1¼", Ivory, rayon

Tulle: 8½" square, Cream

1 Refer to General Dyeing Instructions on page 12 and Dye Recipes on page 78. Prepare dye bath and dye flower Rusted. Let dry. For an alternative method, paint flowers with watered-down Rust acrylic paint. **2** Gather-stitch all edges of tulle, rounding corners. Pull slightly so tulle begins to cup. Fill with potpourri. Pull thread as tightly as possible and knot. **3** Place doily on work surface, right side down. Gather-stitch around edge of doily, 1" to 1½" from outer edge. Place tulle ball onto doily center. Pull thread as tightly as possible to enclose tulle ball and knot. **4** Tie ribbon around gathers into bow. Adhere flower over bow.

Sweater Vest

Supplies

Crocheted flowers: (42) 3", Beige; (22) 2", Beige

Fiber-reactive dyes: (.2 oz. each) Koala Brown; Leaf Green; Mexican Red; (.3 oz.) Black; (.6 oz.) Ultraviolet

Lace doilies: (2) 8" round, Beige, crocheted; 20" square, Beige, crocheted

Lace flowers: (21) 5" x 4", Beige, Belgian

Lace placemats: (3) 14" x 20", Beige, crocheted

1 Refer to General Dyeing Instructions on page 12 and Dye Recipes on page 78. Prepare dye baths. Dye lace flowers Chocolate. Place eight 2" crocheted flowers in a net bag. Dye all remaining pieces , including those in net bag, Plum. Remove net bag after 30 minutes and continue dying remaining pieces. Press all items while slightly damp. **2** Refer to Vest Assembly Diagram on page 93. Sew or hand-stitch 20" edge of one placemat to edge of square

doily, overlapping edges about 1". This forms the vest back and back yoke. Overlap one 8" round doily to left and one to right sides of remaining 20" edge of placemat. This will form front yoke. Underlap and sew or hand-stitch 14" edge of one placemat under 8" doily, on both left and right sides, forming the left and right vest fronts and vest lapels. **3** Fold front placemats over 20" square doily, with right sides together, and align scallops at sides. Sew five of the scallops together from bottom to top, forming the vest side seams. **4** Refer to Lapel Assembly Diagram below. Fold left and right fronts down diagonally at neck edge to form lapel. Pin crocheted flowers onto lapel and back yoke, beginning with 3" flowers, as shown in diagram. Continue to back neck edge, over- or under-lapping doilies and building lapel with doilies. When pleased with placement, hand-stitch all doilies in place. Add one 4" x 5" flower to each left and right front

lapel. **5** Make ½"-deep tucks in scallops at armhole openings so that armhole shape is not floppy. Hand-stitch tucks in place. Pin and hand-stitch five 2" flowers under six 3" flowers to each armhole, beginning at yoke front and continuing around to back. **6** At hem, overlap 4" x 5" flowers over vest bottom edge. Hand-stitch in place. Pin and hand-stitch 3" flowers between 4" x 5" flowers.

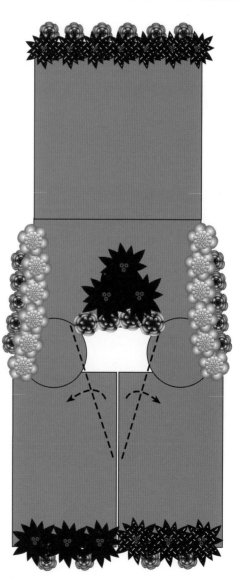

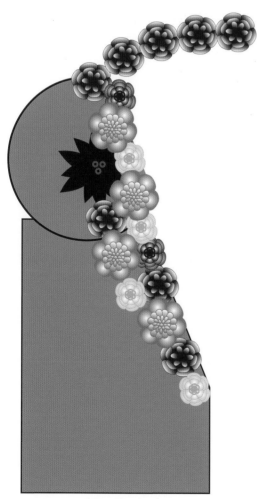

Lapel Assembly Diagram

Vest Assembly Diagram

A Place of Solitude

Decorating is a state of mind, a cherishing of time and place, and an opportunity to create from what is found, what is cherished, what is new. The home and your quiet private place in it, become a place for self-expression, a return to elegance and femininity.

One of the blessings of grown-up years is having a place in your home that is just yours. It is this place in your heart that you have filled with treasures—some your own, some your grandmothers, re-dyed and remade.

You will never cease longing for the precious hours you spend in your not-so-secret, but private place, where imagination has room to grow, where dreams find wings, and where you will find a special solace and peace.

Backpack

Supplies

Backpack pattern

Cording: (1¼ yd.) ⅛", Beige

Fabric: (1 yd.) 44"–54"-wide, Dark Rose, moire

Gimp: (1 yd.) ½"-wide, Beige

Lace doilies: 6", Beige, Battenburg, round; 6", Beige, ribbon lace, round; various

1 Cut out backpack pieces from fabric, using pattern. Assemble flap. **2** Refer to Overlapping Laces on page 22. Sew various doilies onto fabric pieces as desired. Sew Battenburg doily over flap. Sew ribbon lace doily over Battenburg doily. **3** Finish backpack, using cording for drawstring and gimp for shoulder straps, following pattern instructions.

Window Drape

Supplies

Lace table runner: (2) 16" x 72,
Beige, filet crochet

Lace trim: (1 yd.) 4"-wide,
Beige, filet crochet

1 Fold one table runner under 4" lengthwise. Sew 1½" from folded edge, to form rod pocket. On second table runner, fold under 24" widthwise. Sew 1½" from folded edge to form rod pocket. **2** Insert curtain rod through rod pockets beginning with horizontal curtain. Hand-gather bottom and top of vertical curtain, so it drapes gracefully.

Small Heart Wreath

Supplies

Acrylic paints: Peach; Rose

Brass charms: antique finish, butterfly; antique finish, dragonfly

Cording: (¾ yd.) ⅛"-wide, Gold Metallic

Crocheted flowers: (4) 3", Beige; (12) 2", Beige

Lace Doily: 4", Beige, tatted

Porcelain angel head: 3" x 1½"

Ribbon: (½ yd. each) 4 mm-wide, Blush, silk; 4 mm-wide, Café, silk; (1½ yds.) 1"-wide, Ivory; (1 yd. each) 1½"-wide, Golden Mauve, sheer; ⅝"-wide, Gold-edged Taupe, sheer

Seashells: (3) ¾"

Stencil brush: ¾"

Wire form: 6"-diameter heart

1 Wrap 1" ribbon around wire form, covering wire completely. **2** Using stencil brush, lightly paint the center of eight 2" flowers Peach and Rose. Knot cording 2" from one end. Trim opposite end just past knot. Adhere knot to center of one painted flower, leaving 2" end loose. Gather flower around cording and secure with thread. Fray cording ends, creating stamens. Repeat, making seven gathered flowers with stamens. **3** Adhere one gathered flower to center of one 3" flower. Repeat, making a total of four gathered, double layered flowers. **4** Gather center of doily. Adhere doily to heart top center. Adhere flowers around heart as desired. Refer to Folded Leaf on page 25. Make ten folded leaves from ⅝" ribbon. Adhere leaves among flowers. Drape 1½" ribbon across heart back and sides, adhering ribbon in place. Adhere seashells to heart as desired. Tie a small bow with both 4 mm ribbons. Adhere bow to wreath and knot ends. Adhere bugs and angel to wreath with industrial adhesive.

Heart-shaped Purse

Supplies

Lace doilies: (2) 6", Beige, tatted, heart; 6", Beige, Belgian lace, heart; 6", Beige, Battenburg, round

Crocheted flowers: (2) 3", Beige; (3) 2", Beige

Fabric: 12" x 7", Beige, silk jacquard

Cording: (1 yd.) ¼", Ivory

Stamens: (1 bunch) Ivory

1 Place tatted doilies wrong sides together. Place bottom point of Belgian lace doily 1½" between bottom points of tatted doilies. Sew tatted doilies together at sides, catching Belgian lace doily, leaving tatted heart tops unstitched, forming purse front and back. Trim excess Belgian lace doily from inside purse seam. **2** Using purse as a pattern, cut lining front and back from fabric, adding ½" seam allowance to sides and top edges. With right sides together, sew lining sides, turn right side out. **3** Turn down lining straight edge ½" to right side. Slip lining into tatted hearts and align lining straight edge 1" from heart top edges. Sew lining in place. **4** Cut Battenburg doily in half. Sew cut edge of doily to purse back top edge, just above lining straight edge. Sew, taking a ¼" seam. **5** Sew ends of cording to purse front top edge underneath front flap. Fold purse front flap down and press in place. **6** Sew 2" flowers to purse top at sides and purse bottom point. **7** Sew or adhere stamens to center of one 3" flower. Refer to Doily Rosette on page 25. Make rosette and sew to center of remaining flower. Sew flower to purse flap.

Miniature Dress Form

1 Center and sew or adhere 8" heart doily to dress form bodice back at shoulders, bringing some of doily to front. Repeat with 6" heart doily on dress form bodice front. **2** Cut a 10"-diameter circle from center of tablecloth. Gather-stitch around center cut edge. Slip tablecloth over dress form through hole, resting at waist. Pull gather thread to fit snugly at waist and knot. Overlap two 6" Battenburg doilies about 3". Gather-stitch 1¼" from one overlapped edge. Pull thread so doilies measure 5" and knot. Trim doilies ½" from gathered edge. Repeat with remaining 6" Battenburg doilies, forming left and right "peplums". Sew or adhere peplums to left and right sides of waist, leaving 1" gap at waist front. **3** Gather-stitch an 8"-wide center section on skirt front, placing stitches 3" from bottom edge. Tightly pull thread and knot. Tack some of gathered skirt to dress form bottom, so skirt front cups up, creating a train at skirt back. **4** Trim away center from remaining 8" doily. Slip doily over top of dress form, resting trimmed edge on bodice shoulders. Sew to dress form. Drape 6" round crocheted doily over dress form top so finished doily edge meets cut edge of 8" doily. Sew in place. Gather-stitch around doily at neck and pull gathers tight so that it fits snugly to neck. Knot thread. **5** First, make 2"-wide flat bow from Dark Purple ribbon and set aside. Cut two 9" lengths from Dark Purple ribbon. Tuck and sew one end of each length under left and right edge of 6" heart doily at waist. Wrap ribbons snugly around waist and tie into bow. Make a four-looped bow with remaining Dark Purple ribbon. Make a seven-looped bow from Variegated Ombre ribbon. Adhere both bows to waist back, forming a bustle. **6** Refer to Embellishments on pages 24–27. Make flowers from

Supplies

Dress form: 20" tall, with stand and fabric covering

Lace tablecloth: 36", Beige, Battenburg, round

Lace doilies: 8", Beige, Cluny, round; 8", Beige, crocheted, heart; (4) 6", Beige, Battenburg, round; 6", Beige, crocheted, heart, 6", Beige, crocheted, round

Ribbon: (1½ yds.) 1½"-wide, Dark Purple, wired; (2 yds.) 1½"-wide, Variegated Ombre, wired; (12") 1"-wide, Burgundy/Green/Ombre, wired; (1 yd.) ³⁄₁₆"-wide, Dark Brown, velveteen

Braid: (12") ⅛"-wide, Plum

remaining ribbon as desired. Adhere flowers to waist front. **7** Snugly wrap two rows of narrow braid around neck. Adhere to neck back. Adhere flat bow over braid at back. Adhere flower to neck front.

1 Cut out vest fronts, back, and collar lapels from Gold Metallic fabric and Ivory fabric (for lining), using pattern. If applicable, make darts in vest fronts and back. **2** Refer to Overlapping Laces on page 22. Place doilies on vest fronts and vest back as desired. Lace pieces should look as though they belong together, as with a piece of lace yardage. Cut and use portions of doilies as needed. Overlap doilies ¼" and trim away excess. Save all scraps to be used elsewhere in lace collage. Sew doilies in place on vest front and back. Be certain that any trimmed edge underneath a finished edge is caught when sewing. **3** Refer to Lapel Pattern, on page 105, Embroidery Stitch Guide below, and Lapel Stitch Diagram on page 104. Copy and transfer Lapel Pattern onto Lapels. Embellish and embroider lapels, keeping all work ¼" from collar seam line. Hand-stitch flowers in place. **4** Refer to Embellishments on pages 24–27. Make ribbon leaves and flowers with ribbon as desired. Drape gold metallic cording on lapel and hand-tack in place. **5** Finish vest, following pattern instructions.

Supplies

Cording: various

Crocheted flowers: (2) 3", Beige; (8) 2", Beige

Fabric: (1¼ yd. each) 44"-wide, Metallic Gold; 44"–54"-wide, Ivory, moire

Lace doilies: various, Beige

Ribbons: various

Vest pattern

Embroidery Stitch Guide
(Refer to Lapel Stitch Diagram on page 104.)

Step	Ribbon	Stitch
1	4 mm Blush	Bullion Lazy Daisy
2	4 mm Bronze	Lazy Daisy
3	4 mm Olive	Ribbon Stitch
4	4 mm Old Gold	Ribbon Stitch
5	4 mm Light Olive	Ribbon Stitch
6	4 mm Blackish Purple	Colonial Knot
7	3 mm Textured Heather	Ruched Ribbon Stitch
8	Narrow cording	Bullion Lazy Daisy

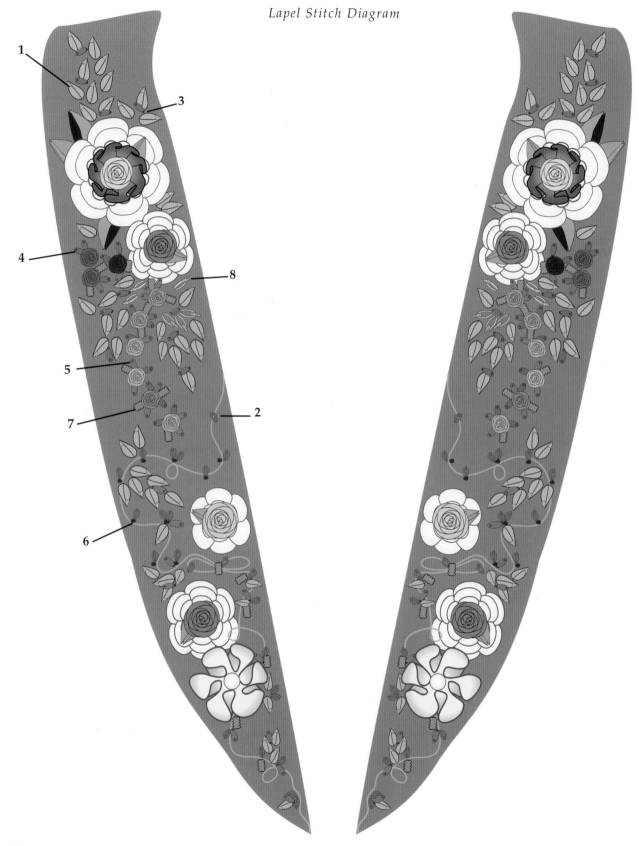

Lapel Stitch Diagram

Lapel Pattern

Enlarge 200%

Stitch-in-Time Frame

Supplies

Embellishments: assorted beads, small buttons, brass charms, pearls

Fabric: 9" x 11" Peach cotton; 8" x 10" fleece

Frame: 8" x 10"

Lace: assorted scraps

Mat board: 8" x 10"

Ribbon: (¾ yd. each) ⅛"-wide, Cream; ⅛"-wide, Mauve; (½ yd. each) ⅛"-wide Tan; ⅛"-wide Yellow; ¼"-wide Pink, cut in half

Silk embroidery floss: Light Green; Pink; Tan

1 Cut fleece to cover mat front. Repeat with Peach fabric, adding 1" to all sides and clipping inside corners. **2** Adhere fleece to mat board front with craft glue. Center front, fleece side down, on wrong side of Peach fabric. Fold edges to back and adhere. Refer to Overlapping Laces on page 22. Hand-stitch lace scraps to mat board front as desired. **3** Refer to Embellishments on pages 24–27. Make one Rosette from each ⅛" ribbon color and adhere to mat board front as desired. **4** Tie a small bow from one 17" length of Cream ribbon. Tack or adhere to top left corner of mat board window. Repeat with one 9" length of Pink ribbon. Tack or adhere to bottom center of window. Make bows with remaining ribbon as desired. **5** Adhere assorted embellishments to mat board front as desired, following designs in lace. Embroider with floss as desired.

A Place to Celebrate the Season

The most wonderful memories are created by the times shared, the meals prepared, the joyful colors, the fanciful decoration, and the peaceful places of a home during the holiday season. An attitude of decorating that celebrates the seasonal proclamation of friendship, celebration, and love. The true celebrations of the season can be found in its simple pleasures. The warmth of a fireplace with its mantel and hearth draped in lace and a traditional tree adorned with angels or Santas from a more Victorian time are the remembrances of traditions that make a home so cherished and memorable during the holidays.

Dye Recipes

▪ Old Green ▪	▪ Sage Green ▪	▪ Red ▪
	Leave in dye bath 30 minutes	
.2 oz. Black	.1 oz. Sea Green (8 oz. mixed)	.2 oz. Koala Brown
.4 oz. Tartan Green	.1 oz. Tartan Green (8 oz. mixed)	.4 oz. Purple Vine
.2 oz. Turquoise Saga		.4 oz. Mexican Red
Used with Lap Throw on page 125.	*Used with Lap Throw on page 125.*	*Used with Lap Throw on page 125.*

General Ornament Supplies

Acrylic paints: Cream; Metallic Gold; Pearl White

Container: small, plastic

Embossing powder: Clear

Glitter: Iridescent, ultrafine

Heat gun

Spray adhesive

Stencil brush: ¾"

Tacky glue: thick-bodied

General Ornament Instructions

1 Press all lace items prior to use. **2** Be certain to work on a protected work surface. A paper bag torn open at the seams makes an excellent drop cloth and provides for simple and quick clean-up. Pour embossing powder into a small plastic container, large enough to hold the item to be embossed. Set up heat gun. **3** For items that are painted, use stencil brush to paint right side of piece with a light coat of Pearl White paint. Some pieces will also be painted on back sides. **4** For items that are embossed, place wet painted piece into container with embossing powder. Cover and shake container from side to side to coat item. Tap off excess embossing powder, then use heat gun to melt embossing powder onto lace. Set aside to dry. Be certain to emboss pieces immediately after paint has been applied. **5** Thick-bodied tacky glue works best for ornament assembly. It adheres as quickly as hot glue, although it will require a longer setting time. **6** After assembling, lightly coat ornaments with spray adhesive, then sprinkle with glitter.

Table Wreath

Supplies

Acrylic paint: Metallic Gold; Pearl White

Artificial foliage: various

Florist wire

Grapevine wreath: 12"

Lace angels:(2) 6", White, starched; 5", White, starched

Spanish moss

1 Paint angels Metallic Gold. Dab Pearl White paint lightly over Metallic Gold. Let dry. **2** Attach angels to top of wreath with florist wire. **3** Attach foliage to wreath as desired. **4** Adhere moss to wreath as desired with tacky glue.

Birdhouse Ornament

Supplies

Birdhouse ornament: 2¾" x 3" x 1¾", papier maché

Cording: (8") Gold, fine

Crocheted flowers: 3", Beige; 2", Beige

Lace trim: (6") 1¼"-wide, White, Cluny

1 Refer to General Ornament Instructions on page 110. Paint birdhouse Cream. Let dry. Repeat. Paint with thin coat of Metallic Gold. **2** Paint and emboss right sides of flowers and trim. **3** Adhere trim around bottom half of birdhouse. Adhere 3" flower to roof. Adhere 2" flower to bottom of birdhouse. Adhere loop of cording to top of ornament for hanger.

Shown from left to right Birdhouse Ornament; Santa Ornament on page 115; and Snow Girl Ornament on page 114. Snowflake Ornament(s) on page 121 are shown throughout photo.

Snow Girl Ornament

Supplies

(for one)

Cording: (8") Gold, fine

Crocheted flowers: (1) 3" Beige;
(4) 2" Beige

Lace trim: (3") 1¼"-wide, White,
Cluny

Paper face: 1" x 1¼"

Ribbon flower: 1", Ivory, rayon

Snowman ornament: 2" x 6",
wooden

1 Refer to General Ornament Instructions on page 110. Paint ornament Cream. Let dry. Repeat. **2** Paint and emboss right side of 3" flower, one 2" flower, and trim. **3** Fold remaining 2" flowers in half, wrong sides together and adhere at edges with tacky glue. Adhere folded edge tip of each unpainted flower vertically to each side of ornament's middle section, for arms. **4** Adhere wrong side of 3" flower to front bottom section of ornament. Adhere painted and embossed 2" flower to front of ornament's middle section, covering where arms have been adhered. Wrap and adhere trim around ornament's hat. Adhere remaining unpainted 2" flower to top section of ornament. Center and adhere face to flower on top section. Adhere ribbon flower to top of ornament. Adhere loop of cording to back of ornament for hanger.

Santa Ornament

Supplies

Ball knob: 2½", wooden

Cording: (8") Gold, fine

Lace cone: 6", White, starched

Paper Santa face: 1½"-diameter

Ribbon: (6") 2½"-wide, Gold, krinkle, sheer

Ribbon flower: 1", Ivory, rayon

Yarn: Cream, slubby (or 1 package doll hair)

1 Refer to General Ornament Instructions on page 110. Paint cone Pearl White and emboss. When dry, twist cone to form beard shape and set aside. **2** Adhere face to ball with tacky glue. Adhere yarn in rows, covering entire ball except face. Adhere ball to top of cone. Drape and adhere five rows of yarn to sides of head to form Santa beard. **3** For Santa cap, remove wire from ribbon, if applicable. Adhere cut ribbon ends together, forming a seam. With seam at center back, adhere ribbon to top of head for cap. Gather-stitch top edge of ribbon, then pull gathers as tight as possible and knot thread. Before cutting thread away, pull gathered cap end to right side of cone and tack in place. Adhere flower over gathered edge where cap meets cone. Adhere loop of cording to back of ornament for hanger.

Finial Ornament

Supplies

Cording: (8") Gold, fine

Crocheted flower: 3", White

Finial ornament: 2½" x 6½", papier maché

Lace trim: (9") ¼"-wide, White, tatted

Ribbon flowers: (16) 1", White

1 Refer to General Ornament Instructions on page 110. Paint ornament Cream. Let dry. Repeat. Paint ornament Metallic Gold. **2** Paint and emboss right sides of 3" flower and trim. **3** Wrap and adhere 3" flower around bottom section of ornament. Evenly space and adhere eight ribbon flowers to top of ornament. Repeat for a second row beneath first. Adhere trim to middle section of form. Adhere loop of cording to top of ornament for hanger.

From left to right are Ball Ornament on page 118; Finial Ornament above; Heart Ornament on page 118. Snowflake Ornament(s) on page 121 are shown throughout photo.

Ball Ornament

Supplies

Ball ornament: 2½", papier maché

Cording: (8") Gold, fine

Lace doily: 8", Beige, Cluny, tatted,
 or Tuscany

1 Refer to General Ornament Instructions on page 110. Paint ornament Cream. Let dry. Repeat. Paint ornament with thin coat of Metallic Gold. Let dry. **2** Gather-stitch around doily ¾" in from edge. Place doily, wrong side up. Place ornament on doily center. Pull gathers as tight as possible so doily cups tightly around ornament, with ornament hanger extending out from the center of gathers. Wrap thread several times around gathered edge of doily and knot. Adhere loop of cording to top of ornament for hanger.

Heart Ornament

Supplies

Cording: (8") Platinum, fine

Gimp: (½ yd.) ¼"-wide, Ecru, scroll

Heart ornament: 2½", Clear

Lace doilies: (2) 4", Beige, Cluny or reticella

Ribbon: (24") ⅝"-wide, Platinum

1 Refer to General Ornament Instructions on page 110. Paint right sides of doilies Pearl White. Let dry. **2** Center and adhere one doily to half of ornament, extending doily to ornament side seam. Repeat with second doily on remaining side. Adjust outer doily edges so they ruffle evenly. Let dry. **3** Adhere gimp to both doilies at sides of ornament. Tie two bows with ribbon. Adhere one bow to each doily at top of ornament. Adhere loop of cording to top of ornament for hanger.

Clear Ball Ornament

Supplies

Ball ornament: 2½", Clear

Cording: (8") Platinum, fine

Gimp: (½ yd.) ¼"-wide, Ecru, scroll

Lace doilies: (2) 6", Beige, Cluny or reticella

Ribbon: (24") ⅝"-wide, Platinum

1 Refer to General Ornament Instructions on page 110. Paint right sides of doilies Pearl White. Let dry. **2** Center and adhere one doily to half of ornament, extending doily to ornament side seam. Repeat with second doily on remaining side. Adjust outer doily edges so they ruffle evenly. Let dry. **3** Adhere gimp to both doilies at sides of ornament. Tie two bows with ribbon. Adhere one bow to each doily at top of ornament. Adhere loop of cording to top of ornament for hanger.

Angel Ornament

Supplies

Cording: (8") Gold, fine

Crocheted flower: 2", Beige

Lace angel: 5", White, starched

Lace doily: 6", Beige, Cluny

Ribbon: (12") ⅝"-wide, Brandished Gold

Ribbon flower: 1", Ivory, rayon

1 Refer to General Ornament Instructions on page 110. Paint angel Metallic Gold. Sponge Pearl White lightly over Metallic Gold. **2** Trim 2" from center of doily. Paint right side of doily and 2" flower Pearl White. Gather-stitch center of doily. **3** Slip angel through center of doily to waist. Pull gathers as tight as possible and knot thread. Wrap gold ribbon around waist and tie in bow at front. Adhere 2" flower to top of head. Adhere 1" flower to center front of bodice. Adhere loop of cording to top of ornament for hanger.

Snowflake Ornament

Supplies (for one)

Cording: (8") Gold, fine

Lace snowflake: 3", White, starched

1 Refer to General Ornament Instructions on page 110. Paint snowflake Pearl White and emboss both sides. Let dry.

2 Twist snowflake "arms" to enhance shape. Adhere loop of cording to top of ornament for hanger.

From left to right are Clear Ball Ornament on page 119; Angel Ornament on page 119; Star Tree Topper & Ornament on page 122. Snowflake Ornament(s) are shown throughout photo.

Star Tree Topper & Ornament

Supplies

Cording: (8") Gold, fine

Lace doilies: 4", Beige, reticella; 6",
Beige, Cluny; 8", Beige, reticella;
10", Beige, Cluny

Ribbon flower: (2) 1", Ivory, rayon

Star ornament: 5", papier maché

Star tree topper: 10"

1 Refer to General Ornament Instructions on page 110. Paint tree topper and ornament Cream. Let dry. Repeat. Paint with thin coat of Metallic Gold. **2** Paint right side of doilies Cream. Paint back side scalloped edge of 6" and 10" doilies. **3** Center and adhere 4" doily to ornament. Gather-stitch a 2" circle around center of 6" doily. Pull gathers tightly and knot thread. Trim away excess lace from gathered center. Adhere doily to back of star. Adhere ribbon flower over gathered center of doily. Repeat for topper, replacing 4" doily with 8" doily and 6" doily with 10" doily. **4** Adhere loop of cording to top of ornament for hanger.

Toddler's Jacket

Supplies

Buttons: (4) ¾" x ½", Bronze, pinecone

Fleece: (1 yd.) 54"–60"-wide, Navy/Teal plaid

Jacket pattern: with pockets

Lace collars: (3 sets) 2"-wide, Beige, Irish Rose

1 Cut and sew toddler's jacket from fleece, following pattern instructions. **2** Press lace collars. Pin each side of one collar set to inside neck edge, placing collar ¼" below inside finished neck edge. Hand-stitch straight edge of collar in place. Fold collar over neck edge to right side of jacket. **3** Pin one lace collar to outside of each sleeve, about 1¼" from hemmed edge. Hand-stitch straight edge of collar in place on sleeves. **4** Using third collar set, cut one collar in half. Pin a collar half to top edge of pocket, folding some of collar to inside of pocket and folding under cut edge on outside of pocket. Hand-stitch collar in place along all edges. Repeat with second collar half and pocket. **5** Hand-stitch buttons in place on jacket front.

Lace-collared Teddy Bear

Supplies

Cording: (1⅛ yd.) ⅜", Burgundy, chenille

Lace collar: 5"-wide, Beige, crocheted

Teddy bear: 18"

1 Press lace collar. Gather-stitch along straight edge of collar ¾" in from edge. Place collar around neck and pull gathers as tight as possible. Knot thread. Tack collar in place. **2** Tie cording in bow around neck. Knot cording ends.

Lap Throw

1 Refer to General Dyeing Instructions on page 12 and Dye Recipes on page 110. Prepare dye baths. Dye doilies Old Green, Sage Green, and Red as desired. Press while slightly damp. 2 Crochet Navy border around each doily on scalloped edges. Hand-stitch doilies together into rows with yarn. 3 Hand-stitch rows together with yarn. Press rows. 4 Crochet border to flat edge of trim. Hand-stitch crocheted edge of trim to border of throw with yarn.

Supplies

Fiber-reactive dyes: (.1 oz.) Sea Green; (.2 oz. each) Black; Koala Brown; (.4 oz. each) Purple Vine; Mexican Red; Turquoise Saga (.5 oz.) Tartan Green

Lace doilies: various square, White, crocheted

Lace trim: (to fit) 4"-wide, Beige, filet crochet

Yarn: (to fit) Navy

Acknowledgments

We would like to offer our sincere appreciation of the valuable support given in this ever-changing industry of new ideas, concepts, designs, and products. The projects shown in this publication were created with the outstanding and innovative products developed by:

The Cotton Ball
475 Morro Bay Blvd.
Morro Bay, CA 93442
cottonball@thegrid.net

Decorator and Craft Corp.
428 S. Zelta
Wichita, KS 67207-1499

**Designs by Joy
Professional Machine
Quilting Services**
PO Box 1435
Morro Bay, CA 93443-1435

Handler Textile Corp.
24 Empire Boulevard
Moonachie, NJ 07074
www.htc-handler.com

Mill Hill
3930 Enterprise Drive
Janesville, WI 53547-1060
www.millhill.com

Personal Stamp Exchange
360 Sutton Place
Santa Rose, CA 95407
www.psxstamps.com

*Rubber stamp designs copyright
Personal Stamp Exchange. Used
with permission.*

Prym-Dritz Corp.
PO Box 5028
Spartanburg, SC 29304
www.dritz.com

Quilter's Resource
PO Box 148850
Chicago, IL 60614

Sakura of America
30780 San Clemente Street
Hayward, CA 94544-7131
www.gellyroll.com

Saro Trading Company
720 W. Broadway Street
Glendale, CA 91204
sarotrading@earthlink.net
www.saro.com

Walnut Hallow
1409 State Road 23
Dodgeville, WI 53533
www.crafts@walnuthallow.com

Metric Conversion Charts

Inches to Centimetres
cm—Centimetres

inches	cm	inches	cm	inches	cm
⅛	0.3	10	25.4	30	76.2
¼	0.6	11	27.9	31	78.7
½	1.3	12	30.5	33	83.8
⅝	1.6	13	33.0	34	86.4
¾	1.9	14	35.6	35	88.9
⅞	2.2	15	38.1	36	91.4
1	2.5	16	40.6	37	94.0
1¼	3.2	17	43.2	38	96.5
1½	3.8	18	45.7	39	99.1
1¾	4.4	19	48.3	40	101.6
2	5.1	20	50.8	41	104.1
2½	6.4	21	53.3	42	106.7
3	7.6	22	55.9	43	109.2
3½	8.9	23	58.4	44	111.8
4	10.2	24	61.0	45	114.3
5	12.7	25	63.5	46	116.8
6	15.2	26	66.0	47	119.4
7	17.8	27	68.6	48	121.9
8	20.3	28	71.1	49	124.5
9	22.9	29	73.7	50	127.0

Solid Measures
oz.—Ounces
g.—Grams
16 oz. = 1 lb.
Lbs.—Pounds
Kg.—Kilograms
1,000 g. = 1 Kg.
Ounces to Grams
& Pounds to Kilograms

oz.	g.	Lbs.	Kg.
1	28.35	1	.4536
2	56.7	2	.907
3	85.05	3	1.361
4	113.4	4	1.814
5	141.75	5	2.268
6	170.1	6	2.722
7	198.45	7	3.175
8	226.8	8	3.629
9	255.15	9	4.082
10	283.5	10	4.536
11	311.85	11	4.99
12	340.2	12	5.443
13	368.55	13	5.897
14	396.9	14	6.350
15	425.25	15	6.804

Yards to Metres

Yards	Metres	Yards	Metres	Yards	Metres
⅛	0.11	3½	3.20	6⅞	6.29
¼	0.23	3⅝	3.31	7	6.40
⅜	0.34	3¾	3.43	7⅛	6.52
½	0.46	3⅞	3.54	7¼	6.63
⅝	0.57	4	3.66	7⅜	6.74
¾	0.69	4⅛	3.77	7½	6.86
⅞	0.80	4¼	3.89	7⅝	6.97
1	0.91	4⅜	4.00	7¾	7.09
1⅛	1.03	4½	4.11	7⅞	7.20
1¼	1.14	4⅝	4.23	8	7.32
1⅜	1.26	4¾	4.34	8⅛	7.43
1½	1.37	4⅞	4.46	8¼	7.54
1⅝	1.49	5	4.57	8⅜	7.66
1¾	1.60	5⅛	4.69	8½	7.77
1⅞	1.71	5¼	4.80	8⅝	7.89
2	1.83	5⅜	4.91	8¾	8.00
2⅛	1.94	5½	5.03	8⅞	8.12
2¼	2.06	5⅝	5.14	9	8.23
2⅜	2.17	5¾	5.26	9⅛	8.34
2½	2.29	5⅞	5.37	9¼	8.46
2⅝	2.40	6	5.49	9⅜	8.57
2¾	2.51	6⅛	5.60	9½	8.69
2⅞	2.63	6¼	5.72	9⅝	8.80
3	2.74	6⅜	5.83	9¾	8.92
3⅛	2.86	6½	5.94	9⅞	9.03
3¼	2.97	6⅝	6.06	10	9.14
3⅜	3.09	6¾	6.17		

Liquid Measures
tsp. = Teaspoon
Tbs. = Tablespoon
oz.—Ounces
ml.—Millilitres
3 tsp. = 1 Tbs.
16 Tbs. = 1 cup
1 cup = 8 oz.

oz.	ml.
¼	7
½	15
1	28
2	56
3	85
4	110
5	140
6	170
7	196
8	225
9	250
10	280
11	308
12	340
13	365
14	390
15	420

Index